Give Us This Day
Year 2

GIVE US THIS DAY
Reflections for Each Day of the Liturgical Year

James McKarns

ALBA · HOUSE   NEW · YORK

SOCIETY OF ST. PAUL, 2187 VICTORY BLVD., STATEN ISLAND, NY 10314

Library of Congress Cataloging-in-Publication Data

McKarns, James E.,
    Give us this day : homilies for each day of the liturgical year /
James McKarns.
        p.   cm.
    Contents: v. 1. Year one — v. 2. Year two — v. 3. Saints and
seasons..
ISBN 0-8189-0611-1 (Year One)
ISBN 0-8189-0612-X (Year Two)
ISBN 0-8189-0613-8 (Saints and Seasons)
ISBN 0-8189-0614-6 (Set)
        1. Church year sermons.   2. Sermons, American.   3. Catholic
Church — Sermons.   I. Title.
        BX1756.M3398G58   1991
        251'.02 — dc20   91-7181
                                                                           CIP

Designed, printed and bound in the United States of
America by the Fathers and Brothers of the
Society of St. Paul, 2187 Victory Boulevard,
Staten Island, New York 10314, as part of their
communications apostolate.

Printing Information:

Current Printing - first digit   1   2   3   4   5   6   7   8   9   10   11   12

Year of Current Printing - first year shown
    1991   1992   1993   1994   1995   1996   1997   1998

DEDICATION

These three volumes of homilies for
each day of the liturgical year are dedicated
to the memory of my father: Donald T. McKarns. He
frequently imparted to others didactic stories, wise
sayings and pensive thoughts. His school was the classroom
of nature and each passing season introduced a new teacher.
It was from him I learned many truths and lasting
lessons, which I have used as life-values.
Concerning the preachers of the Gospel, he
often said, "The good ones are those who
give you something to take home."

INTRODUCTION

My seminary professor of homiletics once made a statement which I have never forgotten: "Don't go to the pulpit," he said, "just to say something. Go with something to say." We certainly should always have something to say for our subject matter is lofty and dignified. Listeners are present and disposed to hear sacred ideas that will influence their lives.

Homilies should be rated as some of the most outstanding and inspiring talks in the world. Not only do we speak of the most challenging mysteries of life, but we also have such ideal conditions in which to convey our messages. There is an atmosphere of silence, reverence, pleasant surroundings, and respect. The list of advantages goes on like a litany. So if the homily falls short of this exalted image, and surveys say it often does, where is the Achilles' heel?

We always have to ask, "Did the homilist step into the pulpit with something to say?" I personally have a phobia about boring people, wasting their time by sounding empty. If I come to preach a homily which first has not excited me, how in God's name is it going to excite anyone else? I would prefer to preach without a shirt on my back, than to try to preach without a definite message in my heart. Never yet have I met a person who can stand in front of a congregation and successfully "wing it" without previous preparation.

If you, the reader, can find some inspirations in these pages which will excite and entice your heart to pour forth your own lofty wisdom, then you will have accomplished both your mission and mine.

As a directive for daily homilies let me leave you with a bit of advice from Dale Carnegie. "Find a good beginning and a good ending and put them pretty close together."

Year 2

MONDAY, FIRST WEEK OF THE YEAR
1 S 1:1-8 and Mk 1:14-20

Mark tells us in this passage that Jesus saw Simon and Andrew and called them to follow him. He mentions no previous contacts. The text also says: "They immediately abandoned their nets and became his followers." We are given the impression that this all happened very spontaneously. The same is implied with the sons of Zebedee — James and John. It is clear from other texts, though, that this was not the first meeting of Jesus and his future apostles. Previously John the Baptizer had introduced them to Jesus and they had spent some time with him. No doubt there had also been other meetings. They all had been given time and opportunity to consider becoming disciples and to discuss the matter with their families. This was to be more than a change of employment. They were not being asked simply to substitute one job for another, but to accept a new way of life. Their vocation was a calling to something completely new and total. These men had some previous experience in ministry with John the Baptizer. Their days at sea had also taught them to live by faith. As fishermen, they daily encountered the mysterious deep, the hidden and uncertain. They would use those same skills on the land — so Jesus called them fishers of men.

TUESDAY, FIRST WEEK OF THE YEAR
1 S 1:9-20 and Mk 1: 21-28

The American Management Association recently completed a study on the reasons why certain managers fail. Some stated causes were: (1) They did not know how to or did not want to delegate their authority. (2) They could not organize people under their jurisdiction. (3) They did not know how to organize their own time. These and other factors led to their downfall. But there was one other major cause of failure which was more basic and more serious than all the rest. Their biggest fault was their arrogance. Arrogance is defined as a feeling of superiority manifested in an overbearing or haughty way of relating to others. Jesus was a person of tremendous authority, both over people and over spirits, as is clearly manifested in today's Gospel. Yet, the Lord was always meek and humble of heart — the exact opposite of those who are arrogant. If we can imitate him in his gentleness and humility and allow our authority to be exercised as much from the heart as with our head, then we can hope to be successful leaders and managers, too. We would also be wonderful Christians, living in the true spirit of our divine master.

WEDNESDAY, FIRST WEEK OF THE YEAR
1 S 3:1-10, 19-20 and Mk 1: 29-39

Those who attend early morning Mass should find great consolation in this sentence from today's Gospel passage: "Rising early the next morning, he (Jesus) went off to a lonely place in the desert; there he was absorbed in prayer." Jesus could have slept late and prayed at home, but he didn't. He chose to leave the house to find a quiet and meditative place for prayer. I love the word used to describe his prayerful frame of mind. He was "absorbed" in prayer. We think of a sponge absorbing water until it is saturated. Jesus, in prayer, was saturated with the thoughts, the sentiments and the glory of God. Then, filled with grace and power, he had more than enough to pour out on all he met that day. We come to church and strive to enter into that same kind of quality conversation with God. By being open to whatever God wills for us each day we place ourselves in a position where we are able to absorb the strength we'll need. We often think of prayer in terms of asking, but prayer also entails praise and thanksgiving.

When we pray well we become absorbed in the presence of God and worship in spirit and truth. We need to participate fully in the holy sacrifice of the Mass and not limit our prayer to a quick preparation for communion. We become absorbed in God's eucharistic presence by concentrating on all the readings, prayers and ceremonies. Jesus strongly believed in the power of prayer and gave to it quality time each day.

THURSDAY, FIRST WEEK OF THE YEAR
1 S 4:1-11 and Mk 1:40-45

In ancient times, when a leper was in the vicinity, everyone would scatter. If the leper tried to approach someone for help, that person would normally turn and run. Everyone was afraid of catching that dreaded disease. Lepers in fact had to warn the people when they were near by calling out: "Leper, leper." Mark says that a leper approached Jesus. People must have been watching to see what the Lord would do. Jesus did not run away, so the leprous man knelt in front of him and poured out the hurt in his troubled soul and body. The man wanted to be normal. He wanted to be able once again to walk among his brothers and sisters as an equal. Many times Jesus had cured people from a distance without touching them. He could have done the same in this case. Instead, though, Jesus reached out and touched him. Now Jewish law strictly forbade anyone to do that — this was an unclean person. But Jesus did not actually break the law, for when he reached out his hand in healing, the man was immediately cured. Jesus did not touch an unclean person, but one who had been restored to health. He was a former leper. Now instead of crying out, "Leper, leper," to everyone, the man could shout with joy, "I'm cured." Good news cannot be silenced. Jesus has forgiven and cured us. Let us all shout for joy in our hearts this day.

FRIDAY, FIRST WEEK OF THE YEAR
1 S 8:4-7, 10-22 and Mk 2:1-12

This text from the Book of Samuel was a favorite of the late outstanding Scripture scholar and professor, Fr. Eugene Maly. He labored hundreds of hours over it and related texts, for this was the basis for his doctoral thesis. Fr. Maly supported the view that God did not want the Hebrew people to have a king, for He, himself, wanted to be their only king. The people, however, continued to clamor for a human king, like the other tribes had. The king was to rule over them and lead them into battle. Although Samuel, God's spokesman, was displeased that the people were asking for a king, he was told by God to go ahead and grant their request. At the same time, however, God confided to Samuel that "the people are rejecting me as their king." Israel had a few wonderful kings but, in general, they caused considerable confusion and trouble. Their first one, Saul, was chosen not for his wisdom or past accomplishments, but simply because he was the biggest man they could find. He was king-sized in body but not in mind. He lived a life of torment and envy. Others had similar difficulties and deficiencies. They were not ideal leaders to follow — even into battle. When we rejoice in the fact we are servants of God then we are acknowledging God as our one and only king.

SATURDAY, FIRST WEEK OF THE YEAR
1 S 9:1-4, 17-19; 10:1 and Mk 2:13-17

Mark frequently pictures Jesus walking along the sea prior to some of his major decisions. In Monday's Gospel, he was moving slowly along the water's edge just prior to calling the first four apostles. Now again, in today's Gospel passage, we find Jesus walking along the seashore, looking at the water and meditating. In the midst of the crowd, the Lord spots Matthew (whom Mark calls Levi). Matthew was an outcast in Hebrew society because he collected Roman taxes from the people. That did not keep Jesus from calling him to discipleship. Matthew's response was immediate. His generosity was also admirable — he at once threw a party in honor of the Lord at which he announced his resignation from his tax-collector's post. And he invited to that party a number of his fellow tax collectors. Think of all the wonderful stories, parables, miracles, and sermons of Jesus which Matthew has preserved for us. In our Church liturgy, this formerly hated tax collector is the most read of all the evangelists. Jesus saw him both for what he was and for what he could become. The Lord specifically chose Matthew as one of the original twelve apostles and his choice has been well vindicated. At times, we may feel unworthy of some office because of our background, family, lack of education or past mistakes. But Jesus is the doctor who can heal all that. The Lord has a place for each of us where we can serve him best and be fulfilled.

MONDAY, SECOND WEEK OF THE YEAR
1 S 15:16-23 and Mk 2:18-22

Do many people put patches on clothes today? It seems to me that we wear our garments until they begin to go out of style or look a bit tattered and then give them to the St. Vincent de Paul Society or to Goodwill Industries. Likewise, in modern wine-making, we use bottles instead of skins for containers. Nevertheless, the point is that some things don't mix and match well. Jesus was not concerned primarily about garments and wine but about what ideas we are blending together in our minds and hearts. How do we, for example, blend into our spirituality both the Old and the New Testaments? We love and respect the Hebrew Scriptures, as Jesus did, and we certainly revere the New Testament even more; but sometimes their messages are contrary.

We cannot mix the rigidity of the Law and the mercy of God's grace into one unified spirituality. We do not react to a situation one time from pure faith and the next time from superstition. That is attempting to unite two things that don't mix. We either trust God's love and providence or we don't. We do not wear a garment of fear, patched with faith. We wear a single robe woven of faith, hope and love.

TUESDAY, SECOND WEEK OF THE YEAR
1 S 16:1-13 and Mk 2:23-28

Those who are the youngest in the family can take heart from today's first reading from Samuel. When Samuel seeks a future king from the sons of Jesse, he rejects each one who is presented to him, beginning with the eldest. It was simply taken for granted that David, who was the youngest, would never be chosen king, so his father didn't even invite him to join the group. He is nearly forgotten until Samuel asks Jesse if these were all the sons he had. Jesse's response went something like, "Oh yes, there is one more, but you wouldn't want to waste your time seeing him. He's the baby of the family." David then, at Samuel's invitation, was called in from the fields where he was herding the sheep and was anointed by Samuel as the new king of Israel. We might think in various circumstances that we don't qualify for some particular office or job. We're too young (or old), unskilled, unworthy, or uninvited. Yet we know our qualities and abilities and need to believe in ourselves. We may be the very person the Lord is choosing for some particular role in life. Also, if we are the one choosing others, this text would caution us to judge by the qualities of the person's mind and heart, and not by appearances only.

WEDNESDAY, SECOND WEEK OF THE YEAR
1 S 17:32-33, 37, 40-51 and Mk 3:1-6

The story of David and Goliath is one of the most familiar in the entire Old Testament. When we read it or hear it read, we already know the outcome. Why do we continue to reread it? Not to discover how it ends, but to discover how to act and find courage in the face of overwhelming odds. David was no match for Goliath, and his slingshot didn't assist him nearly as much as being armed with personal confidence and God's grace. David was sent out with the blessing: "The Lord will be with you." That same blessing accompanies us when we leave at the end of Mass. We also go forth to face our giants and heavy problems which are often too large for us to overcome unaided and alone. We often wonder if we can survive, let alone conquer. David's victory encourages us to fight bravely and overcome those obstacles which stand in the way of projects which we feel are noble and good. That's why we read the story — not for David but for us. What invincible giant do we expect to have to face today? How will we arm ourselves for the confrontation? With personal confidence and God's grace.

THURSDAY, SECOND WEEK OF THE YEAR
1 S 18:6-9; 19:1-7 and Mk 3:7-12

Saul was the ruling king and David, his understudy, was most willing to serve the king in anyway. At his young age, David had already laid his life on the line for king and country in his much publicized clash with Goliath. Saul and David could have been the best of friends, but Saul became extremely jealous. The division was occasioned by a victory which David had won over the Philistines, and the people sang this song, "Saul has conquered a thousand enemies," but "David has conquered ten thousand."

Saul was furious and tried to make it 1001, at David's expense. Jealousy has always been the cause of trouble in the world and it is a major ongoing problem today. When two or more are being compared, someone is apt to get jealous. When compliments are offered to two people, if one receives slightly higher praise, the other can be offended. The lesser compliment is often interpreted by the recipient as indirect criticism or rejection. Jealousy affects both men and women. In recent years the press made much ado about some real or at least reputed jealousies among the first ladies in the White House. Barbara Bush wanted no part of it. Speaking on the subject of popularity on *USA Today,* she said, "I don't threaten anyone. I'm just a nice fat grandmother." That sounds like a very healthy mental attitude to me, one that is not likely to give in to jealousy.

FRIDAY, SECOND WEEK OF THE YEAR
1 S 24:3-21 and Mk 3:13-19

One of the many titles by which Jesus was known is "Son of David." Both Matthew and Luke trace the genealogy of our Lord through Joseph back to David, and beyond. Jesus was a Son of David in many more ways than one. For example, like David, he never acted out of revenge. In today's first reading, we see David in an ideal position to destroy King Saul who has been following him with the explicit intent to have him killed. David's companions unanimously urge him to get Saul first, before Saul succeeds in accomplishing his evil mission. David briefly considers the possibility and then flatly rejects the advice of his companions. He spares the life of Saul. One of the major reasons why David does not strike out in revenge is his tremendous respect for the office of the king. Revenge may have some appeal to us, too, especially if we have been mercilessly hounded and hurt by another. Others may encourage us to seek revenge and tell us that it's the wise and proper thing to do. We, however, must make that decision and be prepared to live with it. The fact that David could reject adverse advice, control his revengeful feelings, and manifest such outstanding respect for the office of the king, shows how very well qualified he was to later become the king.

SATURDAY, SECOND WEEK OF THE YEAR
2 S 1:1-4, 11-12, 19, 23-27 and Mk 3:20-21

We are on the scene in today's reading when David learns of the deaths of both Saul and Jonathan. Jonathan had loved David very much and had protected him several times when his father, Saul, had tried to kill him. Now, that both father and son are dead, David totally forgives Saul and laments equally for the two of them. Later, David would be forgiven by God and the people for his dual sins of adultery and murder. Forgiveness, no doubt, would be extended to him so readily because he was most merciful to others who had offended him. David, the poet and musician, composes an elegy on this occasion and sings it in memory of King Saul and his dear friend, Jonathan. We, too, often feel a tremendous surge of respectful love for those who have died. There seems to be a need to praise the deceased. I think this attitude is often generated from a feeling of regret — of thinking we did not love those people enough when they were alive. Think today about your enemies and forgive them, at least in your heart. Think, too, of a very dear friend and voice your feelings of love and appreciation to them now, before it is too late.

MONDAY, THIRD WEEK OF THE YEAR
2 S 5:1-7, 10 and Mk 3:22-30

When we read this passage today, we are struck by the similarities between David and Jesus. When Jesus was a young boy, it's most likely he read the life of David and probably regarded him as his hero. In his preaching Jesus made many references to what David did on various occasions. Although separated by a thousand years, their lives have many parallels. David began his reign when he was thirty years of age, the same age at which Jesus began his public life. Our Lord spent forty days in the desert preparing for his ministry and David ruled his country for a period of forty years. David and Jesus, as mentioned several days ago, came from the same genealogical line and both were kings. The central city in the life of David was Jerusalem, as it also was for Jesus. The tomb of David is located in Jerusalem and is one of the most sacred sites in Israel. Jesus' tomb, also in Jerusalem, is an even more sacred and frequently visited site. It is near to where he was crucified and is now within the protective walls of a large church. Jesus is the Son of David, who redeemed the world in the city of David. This Hebrew King is, therefore, our ancestor in faith and the more we understand and appreciate his life the better we will know Jesus.

TUESDAY, THIRD WEEK OF THE YEAR
2 S 6:12-15, 17-19 and Mk 3:31-35

The Ark of the Covenant is brought into Jerusalem by David. This was a most important event for, by it, David made the city of Jerusalem the center of both worship and national unity. The Ark belonged equally to the people of the North and South, so Israel could now see itself united under the rule of David in Jerusalem. Contained in the Ark were the Ten Commandments and that made it especially sacred. It was the symbol of God's presence. David, therefore, wanted to be both spiritually and physically close to the Ark. Once he was near the Ark, David was unable to contain himself. He started to dance with joy before the Lord and nearly stripped himself naked as he danced and whirled about in a sacred display of genuine spiritual emotion. In God's presence in church today, there are those who are unable to stand or sit quietly. They feel compelled to raise their hands or dance, which can be a very religious way of expressing oneself. When we move, gesture or dance, as part of our religious celebrations, we are offering up sincere worship to God with our entire body — just as David did.

WEDNESDAY, THIRD WEEK OF THE YEAR
2 S 7:4-17 and Mk 4:1-20

Each day our senses of sight, hearing, touch, taste and smell are bombarded with over 10,000 different sensations. These affect our central consciousness in a variety of ways. Most of the feelings they engender are disregarded but some few take root, influence our thinking and mature into ways of acting which can be either good or bad. Jesus presented a lot of thoughts and ideas to the people by way of formal talks, private conversations, parables and miracles. Many listened and then forgot. Some tried to live the lessons that he taught but did not follow through. Then there were those who heard his words, took them to heart and allowed them to change their lives. The Lord tells us that his words are like seeds sown by the farmer. The future life of the seed depends in large part upon the type of ground into which it falls. It is our obligation to properly dispose ourselves to hear the messages of Scripture. Objectively, the spiritual opportunities are the same for all. If God's word can make some people saints, it can make all people saints. The spiritual power at our disposal is tremendous. We could operate at 100% capacity if we would only dispose ourselves to do it.

THURSDAY, THIRD WEEK OF THE YEAR
2 S 7:18-19, 24-29 and Mk 4:21-25

We can all think of many good deeds which could be done for the glory of God and the good of others. David, a thoughtful and sensitive person, thought it would be a wonderful idea to build a magnificent temple for God. Yet the more he pondered the idea and prayed over it, the less he was convinced that it should be built, or that he should be the one to build it. Regardless of how lofty and noble our ideas may be, we need to take our projects to prayer. Maybe God has some other things in mind for us. The action we envision may best be done by another, either now or at a later time. Perhaps there is something more urgent at the moment which we should be doing. David's prayer and pondering revealed to him another course of action. He was an excellent warrior; he should defeat his enemies and bring peace to the country. He was a superb poet; he should compose psalms and verses which would later be sung in the temple. His son, Solomon, would not be a warrior or a poet, but an outstanding architect; he would be the one to build. We all share in what happens if we all do what we do best. David would "build the temple" by setting the stage for Solomon.

FRIDAY, THIRD WEEK OF THE YEAR
2 S 11:1-4, 5-10, 13-17 and Mk 4:26-34

We don't need to read the paperbacks and magazines or watch the soap operas on TV to see sex and violence. It's all around us and we can find plenty in the pages of the Bible. Today's story is a classic and we can perfectly understand all the attraction, fear, conniving and regret which are found here. We have a powerful king, who normally would be on the battlefield but this year remains at home. With time on his hands, he sees a lovely and lonely woman bathing at a nearby house. He can't ignore the beauty of this young lady. She can't reject the invitation of a king. Their rendezvous leaves her pregnant. After unsuccessful attempts to disguise her pregnancy from her soldier husband, his death is plotted by the King and accomplished on the battlefield. David had those sinful seasons in his life as do most people. He repented and often poured out in prayer his grief-filled conscience. Psalm 5l is a famous plea of lament and there are others. Sin took a heavy toll on the sensitive soul of David and the agony never totally departed him. What appears most attractive at the moment can often lead to a lifetime of bitter regret.

SATURDAY, THIRD WEEK OF THE YEAR
2 S 12:1-7, 10-17 and Mk 4:35-41

If we want to see the strength and raw courage of a prophet in action, we could not find a better example than today's story from Second Samuel. Nathan is sent by God to King David. His mission is to encounter the king, face to face, and expose his secret sin. Realize that frequently the prophets who announced adverse news to the king were themselves killed, as though they were responsible for the bad news. Nathan chooses to approach David by way of a parable. He tells of a rich man stealing a pet lamb from a poor man so that he wouldn't have to touch his own flock. David is infuriated. He wants to punish the person, even kill him: ". . . as the Lord lives, the man who has done this merits death." Then the bomb falls. Nathan delivers that well-rehearsed line, "You are the man!" David could be strong and bold as long as his sins were unknown. When they became public, he was disgraced and weakened. Our sins and faults are within us and we are well aware of them, whether they are public or not. The next time we are about to condemn another, we should ask first if we might not be guilty of the very same fault ourselves.

MONDAY, FOURTH WEEK OF THE YEAR
2 S 15:13-14, 30; 16:5-13 and Mk 5:1-20

The man whom Jesus encountered in this Gospel is a really grotesque character, the type mothers would warn their children to stay far away from. Note how bizarre his actions were. He was possessed by an evil spirit and lived among the tombs in the cemetery. His physical strength was such that he could pull apart chains and smash them. The haunting sound of his unearthly screams would send cold shivers down one's spine. In his state of misery, he hacked his body with stones, leaving himself bruised and bloody. This tormented and demented man must have terrified the neighborhood and perhaps would chase people when they came near. Notice that when he ran toward Jesus, the Lord did not run away. Jesus courageously stood his ground and then healed his tortured soul so he would no longer engage in such deranged behavior. This man emerged from the cemetery — from death — and entered into the main stream of life. The Lord's eyes see through our ugliness and his same healing love has touched us all. No matter how ugly or sin-laden we may be, or think we are, there is never reason to despair. In the Lord's healing mercy we still have hope.

TUESDAY, FOURTH WEEK OF THE YEAR
2 S 18:9-10, 14, 24-25, 30; 19:3 and Mk 5:21-43

This famous passage from Second Samuel is vividly graphic, fast moving and violent. It is most of all psychologically devastating for David, for he realizes that he has no choice. He must defeat his "enemy," who is also his own son. He is unsuccessful in achieving victory while still preserving his son's life. Only a parent can appreciate the anguish he felt upon learning of the death of Absalom. Once you picture the tragic predicament of David's son, hanging from a tree with three pikes thrust through his heart, you cannot easily forget the scene. David is reduced to a state of bitter tears. His sensitive, artistic and, especially, fatherly heart broke as we wept over the death of his son, even though Absalom had been trying to destroy him. The Scriptures make it clear that David was not a revenge-seeking person. Another "spiritual Son of David," Jesus, died like Absalom — hanging from a tree between heaven and earth. He, like David, was not revenge-minded. Revenge is never to be a part of our lives. If we constantly think in terms of getting even, we are not acting as sons and daughters of David — or Jesus — or living according to his teachings.

WEDNESDAY, FOURTH WEEK OF THE YEAR
2 S 24:2, 9-17 and Mk 6:1-6

Many people who live in our neighborhood, our city and our state are well-educated and very talented experts in their various fields, yet we often take them for granted. Even though we know of their impressive credentials, they still remain very ordinary to us. Only when they are recognized or rewarded by some outside source do the local people take note. It is often said that you cannot really be considered an expert in anything unless you come from at least 100 miles away. Some of the hometown crowd took notice of Jesus and others were even amazed at the works he could perform, but few had any strong or lasting faith in him or in his words. Their less than enthusiastic response to him provoked Jesus to remark that "no prophet is without honor except in his native place, among his own kindred and in his own house." His own townsfolk ended up the losers, for many blessings and miracles intended for them were not given because of their lack of faith. We should make a concentrated effort to see, appreciate and acknowledge the real qualities and value of those with whom we deal each day. After all, in the neighboring state, they might all be considered experts.

THURSDAY, FOURTH WEEK OF THE YEAR
1 K 2:1-4, 10-12 and Mk 6:7-13

David knows his death is near and so, very peacefully and in a calm tone of voice, he speaks his last words to Solomon, his son and king to be. He had witnessed so much death in his long life; most of those who were very close to him in this world had already gone to their rest. For them he had wept bitter tears, but for himself he does not weep. David does not question why he must die or try to fend off death for a few more days. Wisdom has taught him to accept death as God's will for all, as he expresses to his son: "I am going the way of all mankind." David says nothing about his own future but concentrates on that of the nation. He prays that Solomon will have a very successful reign and encourages him to be faithful to the laws and decrees of Moses. Had David been as faithful to them as he ought, his life, no doubt, would have seen far less sorrow and turmoil. He dies now as an old man, but with the same courage he had as a teenager when he single-handedly conquered Goliath. Death is the giant he now faces. His passing teaches us that there is no sense in being death-denying people. It's far better to accept death as part of life. Jesus has shown us that, for those who believe, life is not ended, merely changed, and when the body of our earthly dwelling lies in death, we gain an everlasting dwelling place in heaven.

FRIDAY, FOURTH WEEK OF THE YEAR
Si 47:2-11 and Mk 6:14-29

Today Sirach gives a type of eulogy in honor of David. It chronologically follows his life from shepherd boy to King of

Israel. Youth and reckless courage go hand in hand. Those were the days of fighting bears and lions, then proving himself superior to a giant. That launched his illustrious military career, his popularity with women, and it set the stage for him to become the future leader of the nation. The eulogy makes mention of David's love of music and his composition of the psalms, many of which he wrote specifically to beautify the divine worship in the sanctuary. Even his sins are alluded to, for they were a part of his life too. How would we write the stories of our lives? Most of us have goals in mind that we would like to accomplish. If they are difficult and lofty, they will not just happen. We'll need to struggle mightily to turn them into realities. Some may think they are unable to achieve worthwhile objectives because they didn't have the proper background, attend the right schools, or live in the correct places. The lives of successful people teach us that there are more ways than one to succeed. No one is perfectly programmed for any office or position. Shepherds can still become kings.

SATURDAY, FOURTH WEEK OF THE YEAR
1 K 3:4-13 and Mk 6:30-34

Imagine God appearing in a dream, promising you anything you want — just name it and it will be yours. That was the proposal made to Solomon in this passage. Solomon requested wisdom. He realized that his youth and inexperience made it difficult for him to rule the people and he needed wisdom to help him make the right decisions. He shows himself to be very wise, already, by making such a request. He also shows his humility by openly admitting that he is "a mere youth not knowing how to act." God was pleased that Solomon requested "an understanding heart" to govern the people instead of gold, or power, or fame. Even though he did not request them, God promised to give Solomon many material blessings in addition to the wisdom he had asked for. Have you ever prayed for an understanding heart? It's not as popular a prayer request as gold, or power, or fame. It is, however, far more precious. Why not pray today for an understanding heart? Consider and meditate on the meaning of those words. We might be surprised to receive what we ask for and much more besides from the eternal generosity of our heavenly Father.

MONDAY, FIFTH WEEK OF THE YEAR
1 K 8:1-7, 9-13 and Mk 6:53-56

Mark paints a very vivid picture of the ministering Jesus. Wherever he goes, he is literally tripping over people who are ill. Families and friends of the sick brought them out of their homes for Jesus to touch. He encounters them along the city streets and even at the crossroads in the country. Think for a moment of the vast number of people who are in hospitals today. At the time of Jesus, hospitals did not exist and the sick had to stay home and be cared for there. We can, therefore, understand the excited activity and expectant hope which Jesus generated, for he came into the vicinity as a kind of doctor. He imparted not only spiritual strength through his preaching and teaching but actual physical healing as well. The sick were brought on bed rolls with the same urgency we might rush a person to the doctor or hospital today. Many of the early hospitals and medical schools were founded under the inspiration and direction of the Church. Today the hospital, like the Church, is doing the work of Jesus by bringing goodness, love and healing to those who are suffering and sick.

TUESDAY, FIFTH WEEK OF THE YEAR
1 K 8:22-23, 27-30 and Mk 7:1-13

Jesus, raised in a very tradition-centered religion, began preaching the message that it's more important to be faithful to the spirit of God than to traditions of human origin. That was a continual point of contention he had with the scribes and Pharisees. Another way of stating the premise is: It's more important to live by the spirit of the law than by its letter. We belong today to a Church which is very tradition-centered. In fact, we often try to "prove" the correctness of some practice by appealing to tradition — saying that such a custom is unchangeable because it goes far back in tradition. Many of the Jewish people today, particularly the Orthodox, still observe the ancient kosher laws in their diets. This applies to both what they eat and how it is prepared. The Lord teaches it's not the food for the stomach which is important but the food for the mind. Our traditions are fine and necessary but not all are to be observed in the same manner. The distinction must always be made between those of human institution and those revealed by God. If the Spirit of God is moving the Church in a way that goes counter to some ancient traditions, we need to follow the Spirit.

WEDNESDAY, FIFTH WEEK OF THE YEAR
1 K 10:1-10 and Mk 7:14-23

Again, Jesus makes reference to clean and unclean foods, the sprinkling of different kinds of foods, and the manner in which they are prepared. Today many people are very knowledgeable about what should and shouldn't be eaten. We used to be mainly concerned about getting too many calories, but now we are equally careful about cholesterol, sodium, etc. More than in times past, we are aware that diet can be a prime factor in promoting good health. A simple diet shared with a good friend, in a peaceful atmosphere, benefits not only the body, but one's entire being as well. It gives energy, hope and an overall sense of well-being. I think we have not yet come to the realization that what we consume mentally also has a profound effect upon our psychic and emotional well-being. Our mental diet can produce within us either virtuous or evil thoughts and desires which lead to good or bad actions. When asked what we'll have for dinner tonight, we normally would be expected to name some kind of tangible food. Even more important is, what kind of intangible spiritual nourishment will we receive at our meal tonight? What will we be consuming mentally and emotionally before we go to bed?

THURSDAY, FIFTH WEEK OF THE YEAR
1 K 11:4-13 and Mk 7:24-30

The lady who approaches Jesus, requesting a cure for her daughter, comes to him in a humble manner both in mind and body. She did not just genuflect or bow, but she literally crouched at his feet. Someone is crouching when the head is bowed and both knees are bent. One could easily observe how very sincere she was about her request. Jesus, somewhat reluctant at first to grant her petition, was overwhelmed by her profound faith. He told her, ". . . be off now! The demon has already left your daughter." When we are serious about getting the attention of the Lord in prayer, we might assume a crouched position. While in that stance we should make our request. A crouched position is the one which a sprinter assumes while waiting for the gun to sound in the 100 meter dash. It's an intriguing extended image, to picture this fine lady coming to Jesus with so much confident faith that she's ready to dash off with the good news once her request is granted. When Jesus told her that her daughter was cured, can't you just see her dashing back home, not so much to verify the cure but to celebrate it? Wouldn't you? So on your mark, get set, go! Tell the world how God has blessed you and your family today.

FRIDAY, FIFTH WEEK OF THE YEAR
1 K 11:29-32; 12:19 and Mk 7:31-37

They brought to Jesus a man who couldn't hear and asked that the hand of God be laid upon him. Jesus extended his healing hand and the man heard his blessing. The man also suffered from a profound speech impediment. That same extended hand of God blessed him and he was cured. The man's speech was now as clear as was the fact that it was Jesus who had brought about the change. The others who had witnessed this dual miracle — those who could already hear well and speak plainly, could not remain silent about what they had seen and heard. Even though Jesus had strictly requested them to remain silent, they shouted loudly and joyfully, in a state of divine excitement. Each day blessings flow from the hand of God which can heal us and help us to solve the many problems we face in living out our lives. In turn, through our hands, blessings and good deeds can be extended to others. Our many natural abilities, which we often take for granted, are really most precious gifts from God. We can all make a long list of blessings and abilities which come to us from the hand of God. Our hearing and speech are tremendously valuable assets, gifts beyond all material measure. Let us use our blessings well to praise God for his goodness, and, when we can, let us pass them on to others.

SATURDAY, FIFTH WEEK OF THE YEAR
1 K 12:26-32; 13:33-34 and Mk 8:1-10

It is simply fascinating that so large a crowd of people would follow Jesus for three days without anything to eat. This attests to the fact that they were completely caught up in the person and the preaching of our Lord. Perhaps, more properly, we should say that they were being fed such a rich and abundant spiritual diet that they forgot their physical hunger. Jesus, though, fully aware of their human as well as their spiritual needs, took care of both. He always ministered to the whole person. Had they been spiritually satisfied and still remained physically hungry for food, then the total person would not have been at peace. It's good to know that the Lord is interested in the whole person. Regardless of how large the crowd and how sparse the food, the Bible states there were always leftovers. It's a sign that God's grace is never depleted. Seven loaves in the hands of the Lord is more than enough to feed any size crowd. Now we are part of the multitude and Jesus continues to multiply the loaves and fish for us. Any of us can minister to the crowd with whatever gifts we have. Faith and grace can multiply them so that there is enough for all. We can do more with a small amount than we might imagine and there will also be something leftover for others.

MONDAY, SIXTH WEEK OF THE YEAR
Jm 1:1-11 and Mk 8:11-13

In the beginning of the letter of James, there is some advice given which may sound strange to us. The apostle is speaking of those who are in the midst of trials and difficulties, and he suggests a secret way to have a better frame of mind in the midst of all these hardships. He says to think of our trials as "pure joy." Whenever a trial comes, instead of complaining and fighting it, we are to rejoice and say, "Oh good, here comes some more pure joy." It does sound foolish, but that's what the Scriptures say. The apostle tells us that the same approach is valid when it comes to getting our prayers answered. The reason that our prayers often go unanswered is that we pray for the wrong things. It is guaranteed that your prayers will be answered if some morning you say, "Dear Lord, send me some sorrows before noon." You'll soon exclaim, "Thank you, Lord, you sure answered that prayer in a hurry." When we always expect our lives to be lived in a peaceful manner and think every good thing should come to us simply because we presented it in prayer, we will continually be disappointed. This text helps us to realize that we can be about as miserable or as happy as we make up our minds to be. A positive attitude can convert many sorrows into joy.

TUESDAY, SIXTH WEEK OF THE YEAR
Jm 1:12-18 and Mk 8:14-21

Many times we hear people say that God really put them to the test, or that God is trying to see how strong they are. Perhaps those people are remembering how God put Abraham to the test over the sacrifice of his son, Isaac. They envision the same thing is happening to them. The fundamentalist TV preachers frequently, in fact consistently, insist that the devil is tempting them and others and trying to lead all people into sin. Is this truly the way it happens? In this passage of James, the teaching is that neither God nor the devil is the source of all our tests or temptations. James says we are tempted by the "tug and lure" of our own passions within us. When we say our troubles come from some powerful mysterious source outside ourselves, what we are saying in effect is that we are not responsible for what we are doing. Reasoning in the same way, some would say that all their problems come from other people. That, too, is absolving ourselves of personal liability and pointing an accusing finger at others. Granted, there are numerous external forces which affect us. What the apostle here is teaching, though, is that the real enemy is within. Am I ready to face myself responsibly without always blaming the devil or other people for my downfalls?

WEDNESDAY, SIXTH WEEK OF THE YEAR
Jm 1:19-27 and Mk 8:22-26

How can we give true worship to God? James tells us in the closing sentence of our reading today. This is true worship: "Looking after orphans and widows in their distress and keeping oneself unspotted by the world." Orphans are very helpless creatures who generally have no one to care for them. Many passages in Scripture attest to God's immense love for the little, helpless ones of the world. Thus the orphans should become one of the primary objects of our concern. Next are the widows. Notice these are the widows who are in distress. Not all, but no doubt the majority of widows at the time of Jesus, were in distress for back then there were no social security programs, life insurance or other death benefits for survivors. The third element of pure worship is to keep oneself unspotted and uncontaminated by the world and artificial values. Someone added, we should not be so concerned about keeping ourselves unspotted by the world that we forget about the orphans and widows. This is true worship. It's broader than our liturgy in church on Sunday. It's happening out on the streets and in society everyday of the week. We are part of it.

THURSDAY, SIXTH WEEK OF THE YEAR
Jm 2:1-9 and Mk 8: 27-33

We might receive a compliment one minute and then a rebuke the next. That's what happened to Peter on the road with Jesus and the other apostles in the neighborhood of Caesarea Philippi. Mark tells the story. Remember, it was from the preaching of Peter that Mark composed his Gospel. Peter shows his humility here by omitting the compliment he received from Jesus and noting his condemnation. Matthew, alone, tells us how lavishly Jesus praised Peter on this occasion, while the other two synoptics record Peter's rebuke. Peter's remark indicates that he knew Jesus to an extent, but did not know the real nature of his role as the Messiah — that he had to suffer and die. When Jesus tells him to get behind him, it doesn't mean he can't bear to look at his face or that he should get out of his sight. It means that he should be a disciple and walk behind the Lord rather than out in front. Peter was anticipating Jesus and telling the Lord what he should do. Also, Jesus didn't need any more negative comments about his approaching suffering and death, especially from a disciple. When we get in line, become disciples, and walk behind the Lord, we get a better idea of what it is to suffer. Each day we are following Jesus on the road to Jerusalem.

FRIDAY, SIXTH WEEK OF THE YEAR
Jm 2:14-24, 26 and Mk 8:34 - 9:1

Here the old debate surfaces in this passage of the epistle of James. Which is more important — faith or works? James says we do not live by faith alone. Faith is the basis of our beliefs, and to that extent it is most elementary. Good works, however, are faith in action. Without them, the faith we have is not vibrant. It is dead. Paul gives a strong argument for the value of faith over works but he is referring to the works of the Old Law uninspired by faith. Works, in Paul's view, meant slavish adherence to the letter of the old ritual laws. These "works" were proclaimed by the Pharisees and people were supposed to observe them in order to be holy. The spirit of the law was regarded as secondary. The term "works" as used by James does not refer to this Old Testament concept but means good deeds and service to neighbor — such as the works of mercy. In this sense, faith and works go together and compliment each other. They are as inseparable as breath and the body. Faith is basic; not verbal faith, but active faith. If faith is truly active faith, it will contain many good works within it. In essence they are one and the same.

SATURDAY, SIXTH WEEK OF THE YEAR
Jm 3:1-10 and Mk 9:2-13

In this passage, James uses striking and graphic images to describe the problems we often encounter in controlling our speech. Note the contrast between the small size of the tongue and the immense damage it can do. If we can control our tongues, we can regulate our entire lives. A strong, thousand pound horse is controlled by a tiny bit in its mouth. A ship with the bulk of over a thousand tons is maneuvered by a very small rudder. A gigantic forest fire is started by one tiny spark from a careless match or a discarded cigarette. So it is with the tongue, James says. In very harsh terms he refers to the tongue as being enkindled by hell fire. It boasts mightily, can not be tamed, and is "a restless evil, full of deadly poison." If we have ever been slandered, falsely accused, verbally condemned, or needlessly picked apart and negatively criticized, we would undoubtedly agree with this passage from James. Finally, the apostle says that the tongue can be deceptive for it both blesses and curses. Today, instead of cursing and condemning, resolve to say only the good things which others need to hear and to always speak the truth gently and with love.

MONDAY, SEVENTH WEEK OF THE YEAR
Jm 3:13-18 and Mk 9:14-29

How can we know if people possess wisdom and understanding? James gives a clue. Observe them to determine if there are signs of arrogance in their speech and actions. If they show no signs of being pretentious, they probably possess what James calls "humility filled with good sense." That is a clear sign you have made contact with a wise person. If people display bitterness in their expressions and demeanor, being motivated by jealousy and selfish ambition, those people do not possess true wisdom. Someone may have a significant degree of intelligence or knowledge, but the apostle says this is not necessarily the kind of wisdom which comes "from above." Those who live with the real "wisdom from above" display lives which are filled with innocence. They exude a spirit of peacefulness and they are sympathetic to the views and concerns of others more than their own. According to these scriptural guidelines, how many of us really possess quality wisdom from above? Today, each of us might monitor our thoughts, speech, and conduct to see if we qualify as wise and understanding persons.

TUESDAY, SEVENTH WEEK OF THE YEAR
Jm 4:1-10 and Mk 9:30-37

No one needs to be reminded that the world is full of conflicts. They exist everywhere — within individuals, families, communities and churches. Severe conflicts between nations continue today, as in the past. Often they explode into devastating wars. Isn't it absolutely pathetic that we, who are supposed to be so cultured, still try to solve our international differences by the wholesale killing of each other? In most areas of life we are modern but here we're as ancient and barbaric as ever; even worse, for now our weaponry is designed for mass destruction. The Apostle James notes that most of the conflicts and tragedies of the world originate from within individuals. Envy leads to fights. Our "inner cravings" do not subside and they generate conflicts within ourselves. We don't get what we desire and so we literally kill someone to obtain it. Murder, it seems, is not lessening but increasing. Jails, security lights, police forces, locks, and all the other crime-fighting equipment and personnel will not stop crime. The reform must take place within the hearts of individuals themselves. Am I personally part of the problem or part of the solution?

WEDNESDAY, SEVENTH WEEK OF THE YEAR
Jm 4:13-17 and Mk 9:38-40

There's an old customary figure of speech which we still occasionally hear repeated today. It's used by some when they speak about their future plans. After stating what they intend to do, they add: "God willing." To think and speak of our future plans in that way shows that we acknowledge the fact that we don't have total control over future events in our lives. If we talked or tried to act as though we could manipulate the future, we would be exhibiting a very arrogant spirit. It would be a sure sign we were both unwise and unrealistic. Our lives, Jesus tells us, are often as unpredictable as the thin white smoke exiting a chimney. He called them vapor clouds. They are pushed and manipulated by every breeze, and after a short period of time they completely disappear. No one has any real assurance of what will happen tomorrow. My plans and appointments may be made far into the future, but chances are when the time comes, they will materialize differently than I now envision. So what are you planning for tomorrow? Remember, circumstances may cause you to revise your thinking. May your future dreams be fulfilled — God willing.

THURSDAY, SEVENTH WEEK OF THE YEAR
Jm 5:1-6 and Mk 9:41-50

Do you agree with the statement, "The rich are to be pitied?" It sounds a bit foolish, doesn't it? Should we pity the rich more than the poor? Not more, but differently. Both groups can be victims, caught in similar sad situations. Jesus says the rich who have placed their ultimate trust in their wealth are to be pitied. The Lord points out how temporal and disappointing riches really are. Wealth can purchase expensive clothing. They may be the best, but eventually they will rot. The wealthy may amass a gigantic pile of silver and gold, but it will ultimately corrode. The most serious charge brought against the rich, in this incident, is the pitifully small wages they paid to their employees. Worse yet, some of the workers didn't even get the pittance which was promised. The poor often worked hard but went hungry and cold because they were never paid. Their money remained hidden in the homes of the rich. In the middle of the night the money cries out. It awakens and condemns the rich who have withheld it (and thus stolen it) from the poor. The unshared wealth chants a kind of mantra — in the inner conscience of the dishonest rich, "Shame on you, shame on you, shame on you." If justice is not observed, true happiness in society will never be achieved.

FRIDAY, SEVENTH WEEK OF THE YEAR
Jm 5:9-12 and Mk 10:1-12

Jesus is on the scene teaching the crowd of people who had gathered around him. The subject matter he is explaining is not mentioned. Note that it was the Pharisees who introduced the topic of divorce in order to put Jesus to the test. The Lord fields the question well, then throws it back at them with a counter query: "What command did Moses give you?" Jesus was well aware of Moses' teaching on marriage and says in essence that God's view of marriage and divorce is stricter than that taught by Moses to the Hebrews. This was one of the "hard sayings" of Jesus which caused some of his disciples to question him even further regarding the matter. Our Lord then went on to say that this ideal can only be realized with the help of God. This was a very complex question in the early Church as it continues to be today. During the first millennium, many of the various problems of divorce, unfaithfulness, annulments and remarriage were handled informally by individual bishops. Then more formal structures for their resolution began to develop in Rome. These reached their zenith in 1917, with the first publication of the Code of Canon Law. The current code (1983) has given back to diocesan tribunals some of the traditional pastoral power for certain annulment solutions. As it was in the time of Jesus, it continues to be a monumental, but not impossible, struggle for the married to remain "two in one" until death.

SATURDAY, SEVENTH WEEK OF THE YEAR
Jm 5:13-20 and Mk 10:13-16

The apostle James offers us a number of spiritual solutions for the many difficulties which surface in our lives. His remedies flow almost like the lyrics of a song. Do you have a hardship, then pray? Are you sick, get an anointing from the Church. Are you in need of a healing, then offer a prayer for another. Do you want to save your soul, then bring another person back from a life of sin. When facing difficulties, we normally give first attention to our own personal troubles and think of assisting others only when we are whole again. Here, it is suggested that many of our problems will disappear more quickly and more completely if we don't over exaggerate them and, instead of fretting over them and ourselves, we concentrate on helping others. Notice how positive in tone these solutions are. We need to have a certain amount of difficulties in life, for through them we are given opportunities to develop. We might think that, if God wants to heal someone, my prayers are not needed, so why pray for a healing? St. James says that the more healing we personally want, the more we should pray for others. It's a concrete example of loving our neighbor as ourselves.

MONDAY, EIGHTH WEEK OF THE YEAR
1 P 1:3-9 and Mk 10:17-27

The dictionary gives various meanings of the word "needle": (1) A piece of metal with an eye on one end and a sharp point on the other; or (2) A slender sharp pointed indicator on a dial. (3) The verb, "to needle," means to tease. The dictionary does not give the biblical meaning of needle. Some Scripture scholars in the past held that Jesus was referring here to a very low and narrow gate in the wall surrounding the city of Jerusalem which, because of its size, was called "The Eye of the Needle." It allowed for the entrance of a child, or an adult who would have to stoop down in order to get through it, and might be compared to the small door in our modern day barns, cut into the larger barn door. When a herd of cattle or large machinery are moved into the barn, the large door, normally on a track, is opened. If people want to enter the barn, the large door remains closed and a small door on hinges is used. Cattle and horses are too large to enter through the small door. Rabbis at the time of Jesus used the figure of a camel going through "The Eye of the Needle" as an example of the impossible. It would be ridiculous for a camel to try to pass through this small gate, especially with bags on its back. It's a picturesque way of saying that the rich will have difficulty entering heaven if they are still carrying their money bags with them.

TUESDAY, EIGHTH WEEK OF THE YEAR
1 P 1:10-16 and Mk 10:28-31

We read the standings of the various ball teams in the daily newspaper. The most important thing we want to know is who's

in first place. We may read, for example, an account of the
Indianapolis 500 Race. There could be an excellent article de-
scribing the 33 cars on the track and how each driver did an
excellent job. We might be told about some of the engineering
advancements being utilized for the first time at this event and the
insights garnered from the race on the manufacture of better and
safer tires. Most of us are not all that interested, though, in this
kind of information. We want to know who was first. Who won the
race? That same thing is true in regard to social standing, wealth,
good looks, success, etc. We want to know who's number one.
Jesus tells us that all these standings are purely temporary. They
will be scrambled, even reversed. The first will be last and the
last, first. It's one of those famous paradoxes like the one where
Jesus states that those who give up the most will have the most.
His closing reminder is that God has no favorites. So, if we think
we are first and will always be, we are living an illusion. Where we
are, first or last, is not nearly as important as what we are. We are
God's children now.

WEDNESDAY, EIGHTH WEEK OF THE YEAR
1 P 1:18-25 and Mk 10:32-45

The radio newscaster told the story of a man from Miami
who sued his church for $800.00 because of blessings he was
promised but did not receive. He had donated that much money
and now wanted it back because he concluded the church had
deceived him into a bad investment since he did not receive his
blessings. An individual from Texas heard of the incident and sent
$800.00 to the church saying he would take the blessings. The
second person believed any charitable gift brought a blessing. It
was not important that the giver receive any personal benefit. In
the letter from Peter today, blessings have not been purchased

with silver and gold but with the priceless blood of Jesus. It is by his blood that we are saved. We need to think of true values in terms other than monetary. A person acquires genuine riches, not according to how much money one possesses, but ". . . by obedience to the truth," as this passage says. Can my faith support the same truths as my intellect? We praise Jesus for investing his life for our salvation.

THURSDAY, EIGHTH WEEK OF THE YEAR
1 P 2:2-5, 9-12 and Mk 10:46-52

Archaeologists say people lived at the present site of Jericho as far back as 7000 B.C. A modern day visitor can easily see why many would be attracted to this pleasant location in the Jordan River valley. The city stands as a life-giving oasis in the midst of the surrounding desert. It was in this fertile, tropical valley that Bartimaeus lived, smelled the fragrant blossoms, heard the baying of the camels and enjoyed the fresh, lush fruit. Yet, he could not appreciate its beauty for he was blind. Mark says that, on this day, Bartimaeus happened to be in the right place at the right time when Jesus passed through his home town. He wanted Jesus to leave behind one more miracle in Jericho — for him. And so he purposefully and prayerfully cried out eight well chosen words: "Jesus, Son of David, have mercy on me." His faith brought sight to his eyes. We can relate to his story for we all, to some degree, live in darkness, doubt and fear. We may have eyesight but lack insight for there are many kinds of blindness. We are encouraged to not sit by idly in the gloomy shadows of despair. Jesus is nearby, so stand up and call out to him. Good things will happen. You'll see.

FRIDAY, EIGHTH WEEK OF THE YEAR
1 P 4:7-13 and Mk 11:11-26

    This first letter of Peter is very pastoral in nature for it encourages the early followers of Jesus to face their daily lives in a very realistic way. It is a type of "no nonsense" communication to those first-century believers that the Christian faith will make serious demands on their lives. The author plainly says there shall be temptations, trials and sufferings, although it's not all one-sided. Glory will also come to all who follow Jesus and there shall be exultant rejoicing. Adversities, though, must come first. This epistle should be read and assimilated by those who think their faith is supposed to always bring them peace and contentment. When hardships occur some think they are being abandoned by God. How did that notion ever originate? Jesus never promised us a rose garden. In the face of daily troubles and persecution there is some good advice offered here — "Remain calm so that you will be able to pray." This day gives me an opportunity to prove I am living in the spirit of Jesus. In the midst of adversity today, I will, with God's help, remain calm so I can pray.

SATURDAY, EIGHTH WEEK OF THE YEAR
Jude 17:20-25 and Mk 11:27-33

    Mark expresses great pride in the words and deeds of Jesus and writes in such a way that his readers, too, will come to admire the dedication, courage and wisdom of the Lord. This passage, today, follows that very powerful section, read yesterday, where we witnessed the Lord condemning the fig tree and aggressively heaving tables around in the temple. These actions certainly had to impress those who were witnesses and no doubt the "Jewish grapevine" was humming with graphic details about those dramatic and unexpected events. Notice that three groups of people now ban together to confront Jesus. Present are the chief priests, the ubiquitous scribes and the elders. Their question about what gives him the authority to do these things is not an inquiry for information. It is a blunt challenge to the Lord. Cleverly, Jesus uses the old technique of answering a question with a question. "Was John's baptism of human or divine origin?" They answer, "we do not know," because they are afraid to take a definite stand. Jesus took a clear stand and acted accordingly. His adversaries had to admire his calm strength. Can I stand up to anyone and say what I believe, regardless of the consequences?

MONDAY, NINTH WEEK OF THE YEAR
2 P 1:2-7 and Mk 12:1-12

The tenants wanted a piece of the vineyard. For it they were willing to maim and kill. It mattered little to them that they were employees only — not owners. Shamefully, they mistreated the messengers and then killed the owner's son. This is the last parable that Mark tells in his Gospel. It's a summation of the mission and fate of Jesus, explaining in parable how the Lord died at the hands of his enemies. Jesus often compared the Church to the vineyard. The vineyard produces wine for all, as the Church gives grace to all. The people, who logically would have taken leadership positions in the Church, i.e., the Pharisees, especially, were rejected. In the past they had engineered the downfall of prophets and now they were plotting against the Messiah. The Gentiles were to take their places in the Christian Church; they will comply with the wishes of the master. Sometimes we, too, begin acting as if we owned the Church, forgetting we are only servants of Christ. What will make us stop being so selfish and self-centered? When we forget who we are and whom it is we serve and begin acting otherwise, we cause "big trouble" in the vineyard.

TUESDAY, NINTH WEEK OF THE YEAR
2 P 3:12-15, 17-18 and Mk 12:13-17

We can hardly comment on this Gospel without some understanding of the civil strife in Israel at the time of Jesus where civil and religious values often clashed head on. Rome, a foreign and pagan power, occupied the country. The Law of Moses forbade the Jews to support either foreigners or pagans. The people, though, were forced to support the occupying Roman powers with their tax money and that created a real conflict of conscience. Current controversial questions of this nature provided excellent ammunition for the Pharisees to fire at Jesus. This verbal encounter was not generated by any sincere quest for the truth, but it was motivated by the desire of the otherwise opposing factions of the Pharisees and Herodians to trap Jesus in a dilemma. If the atmosphere of this meeting had been less hostile, Jesus might have responded in a less humiliating way. Jesus did not favor either paganism or foreign domination. The question here had more to do with the rights of God. And here Jew and gentile alike had equal obligations. All owed him allegiance. Jesus broke through the artificial barriers of race and national origin and opened the Church to all people, including foreigners and pagans and invites us to look at our religious convictions in a new and better way. Think of someone you may have been treating like an outsider. Begin to see that person as a real brother or sister. Be a true Christian and not a Pharisee.

WEDNESDAY, NINTH WEEK OF THE YEAR
2 Tm 1:1-3, 6-12 and Mk 12:18-27

When we have a doubt concerning some situation, it means we lack confidence in that area. To doubt, in one of its archaic meanings, was to fear. In this reading of Paul to Timothy, the apostle is telling his young bishop the reasons he has more faith than fear. This faith, Paul says, will carry him to the final day. He is the eternal optimist. Our faith is also intended to carry us to the end. Recently, I read this little verse about faith and doubt by an unknown author. It says a lot in a very simple way.

Doubt sees the obstacles,
Faith sees the way;
Doubt sees the blackest night,
Faith sees the day;
Doubt dreads to take a step,
Faith soars on high;
Doubt questions, "Who believes?"
Faith answers, "I!"

How often we see the contrasting ways in which different people cope with problems. For some, everything is a problem. Others never seem to be dominated by them. We need to remember: doubt always sees the obstacles, while faith sees the way.

THURSDAY, NINTH WEEK OF THE YEAR
2 Tm 2:8-15 and Mk 12:28-34

Jesus was a teacher who often had an unexpected answer to religious questions. The scribe, who asked the question in today's Gospel, must have been surprised that the Lord's response was the expected one. This person wanted to know the first (i.e., the most important) commandment. It was a common question asked of different rabbis. Jesus replied with the "Shema," which all the Jews knew and recited twice a day. It was as common to them as the Lord's Prayer is to us. The Shema called for a person to love God with all one possessed — heart, soul, mind and strength. Since God is important, powerful, kind and loveable, it's not asking too much to give one's entire love to God. Had Jesus stopped there, he would have received loud applause from the crowd. Jesus, however, added a real challenge by saying we are to love our neighbor with that very same love. He identifies the two commandments as one. The word, love, is the same in each. That's the real challenge of Christianity — loving our neighbor. Our neighbor, unlike God, is not always loveable, yet the commandment is there. To love my neighbor as myself is the most difficult, yet rewarding, part of being a human being and a follower of Christ.

FRIDAY, NINTH WEEK OF THE YEAR
2 Tm 3:10-17 and Mk 12:28-34

In this passage there is a famous statement about the precious value of Sacred Scripture for our daily lives. "All Scripture is inspired by God and is useful for teaching, for reproof, correction and training in holiness . . ." It is said to make us "fully competent and equipped for every good work." Scripture is also supposed to offer reproof, i.e., to rebuke us or express disapproval to what we do and think that's wrong. It is to correct us and lead us in the right direction. We often hear people quoting or discussing their favorite book of the Bible. It's that book which brings them peace and consolation. However, I don't see consolation listed here as an objective of Scripture reading. If we read all the books of the Bible we are certain to encounter some passages we don't appreciate. Maybe our least favorite books are those needed for our reproof and correction. Remember the entire Bible is the inspired word of God, both the palatable sayings such as, "Peace be with you," and the very difficult ones telling us to "turn the other cheek" and give your shirt to the same one who steals your coat.

SATURDAY, NINTH WEEK OF THE YEAR
2 Tm 4:1-8 and Mk 12:38-44

Paul had brought Timothy into the faith and led him on into the ministry. His young convert became one of his most trusted friends. Today's passage is Paul's final advice to Timothy, who is now serving as bishop. Paul encourages him "to stay with the task, whether convenient or inconvenient . . . constantly teaching and never losing patience." In his book, *The Outsider,* Howard Fast describes a similar scene. A young Jewish rabbi is being sent on his first assignment to a Jewish community north of New York City. Just before he departs his superior tells him, "You must love your congregation even when they are least loveable — which can be frequently." Then the old, experienced rabbi adds a final spiritual directive: "Don't expect righteousness or even integrity. You teach it. And don't expect gratitude. It is very precious and in time it will come, but don't expect it." Advice from a parent, a trusted teacher or a close friend can support us through many difficult times. Those people, like Paul, speak from experience. We are wise if we listen to them.

MONDAY, TENTH WEEK OF THE YEAR
1 K 17:1-7 and Mt 5:1-12

Before a person is canonized as a saint, the Church first declares the individual blessed. Today's Gospel tells us nine ways to become blessed in our own personal striving for holiness. We begin by fostering a strong desire for spiritual progress, rather than concentrating on material success. As we move up the ladder, each step becomes a bit more difficult. We accept sorrow, lowliness and develop a real hunger and thirst to acquire a richer and deeper spirituality. Then we move a step higher by showing mercy to others and living in a most wholesome manner. We face more serious challenges when we start playing the role of peacemakers, for it means we will be working with troublemakers. Persecutions, insults and slanders will result because we are doing the work of Jesus, who personally endured all of these. This may ultimately lead us to our premature deaths, but, if so, there is the promise that our reward in heaven will be great. Now we should exert some personal introspection and determine where on the ladder we are at the present time.

TUESDAY, TENTH WEEK OF THE YEAR
1 K 17:1-7 and Mt 5:13-16

In this passage we find the words: "A city set on a hill cannot be hidden. When Jesus spoke them, he must have been thinking of the city of Jerusalem — one of the most famous cities of the world located on a mountain. Because of its lofty location, the Bible frequently speaks of going "up to Jerusalem." Even when someone is traveling from north to south, it's still "up," rather than going down, as we would normally say. Those who are Christians are not to be hidden either. Each one is to be like a city on a mountain, giving direction, light and courage to others. Since baptism is a public sacrament, those who receive it are now public people called to be shining beacons of hope to all around. They are as the mountain city. Everyone who professes belief in Jesus and is baptized is a public person and, as such, witnesses to others a certain light and truth of the Lord. Everything about Jesus was of a public nature. How contradictory it would have been for him to hide his wonderful light under a basket. Then no one would have seen it. Our light is to shine in the same way.

WEDNESDAY, TENTH WEEK OF THE YEAR
21 K 18:20-39 and Mt 5:17-19

It is a very common situation in the Scriptures to find Jesus at odds with the scribes and Pharisees. Accusations between them sometimes reached a fever pitch. In contrast, there is a bond of understanding and peacefulness between Jesus and his disciples, as we would naturally expect. In this passage it is implied that there may have been some confusion or even disagreement between Jesus and his disciples. Consequently, he tells them how they should and should not be thinking. He had been preaching new concepts, especially in the Beatitudes and perhaps they were finding it difficult to understand why he was opposing the Old Testament Law, which they, too, revered very highly. Jesus, therefore, explains that he is not disregarding the Law but fulfilling it. He came to reveal the true meaning of the Old Testament Law. When the Lord refers to it all being fulfilled, that may be a reference to his coming death and resurrection. Our styles of life call us to be honest with ourselves even though we may be confusing to others. We are all called to live in such a way that we do not destroy but fulfill the teachings of Jesus.

THURSDAY, TENTH WEEK OF THE YEAR
1 K 18:41-46 and Mt 5:20-26

One evening a TV executive was eating dinner with his family. During the course of the meal their topic of conversation centered on a certain disagreement which had arisen between him and a fellow worker. His small son listened for a while and then interjected, "Why don't you kill him, Daddy?" The family members told him that was a terrible thing to say. The little boy replied, "That's what they do on television." Had this youngster been schooled as much in today's Gospel as he had been in television, he would have suggested, "Why don't you forgive him, Daddy?" We are not as blunt as this little boy in our speech but our thoughts sometimes may be similar. Some people are doing a lot of thinking about real killing. The daily paper keeps us aware of that. Why aren't we more forgiving? In this sacred passage, Jesus begs us to forgive our brothers and sisters. More than beg, he threatens us with dire consequences if we fail to be forgiving. Maybe we can't always forgive in word or action but all of us can forgive in our hearts. It's real important that we do it.

FRIDAY, TENTH WEEK OF THE YEAR
1 K 19:9, 11-16 and Mt 5:27-32

When a hurricane hits the coast with devastating force, injuring people and destroying property, someone's going to say, "God is trying to tell us something." In the recent California earthquake there were those who interpreted it as God's presence, making people think and repent of their sins. The same is true of major fires and, in fact, most calamities which are observable, powerful and very dramatic. God, according to many people, is to be seen in these tremendous displays of spectacular energy in nature. Today's reading gives a different view. It says God's presence is in the soft and quiet areas of life as much, if not more, than it is in the dramatic. Elijah, a discouraged and persecuted man, was intently searching for God. He discovered him not in the powerful storm, earthquake or fire, but in the very calm and gentle breeze. We should try to see God's presence in ordinary happenings each day. We can see God in the sunrise, in a leaf blowing or a flower blooming, in the voice of a friend, in a tiny bird and in the sound of our own breath.

SATURDAY, TENTH WEEK OF THE YEAR
1 K 19:19-21 and Mt 5:33-37

The year 49 B.C. Julius Caesar was commanding the Roman legions and daily growing in power. Fearing he would gain too much control and take over the country, the Roman Senate ordered him to break up his army. Caesar defied the Senate and instead crossed the Rubicon River in Northern Italy and continued to conquer. It was his first decisive step toward acquiring the future leadership of Rome. Ever since that time the expression "to cross the Rubicon" has meant to make a definite decision or daring step from which there is no retreating. More than seven centuries before Julius Caesar, the young future prophet, Elisha crossed his "Rubicon." When his mentor, Elijah, placed a cloak on his shoulders, he abruptly made a decisive change in his life. He slaughtered the 24 oxen with which he had been plowing and set fire to his wooden plow. The oxen were roasted and fed to the poor. Then he followed Elijah. He had destroyed his past security, leaving nothing to which he could return. Later, Jesus, who certainly had read the life of Elisha, would tell future disciples to sell what they possessed and give it to the poor and then to come and follow him. It takes tremendous faith "to cross the Rubicon."

MONDAY, ELEVENTH WEEK OF THE YEAR
1 K 21:1-16 and Mt 5:38-42

In 1939, John Steinbeck's historical novel, *The Grapes of Wrath* was published. It became one of the most famous books of our time. In it he traced the "Okie" migration to California during the severe depression of the 1930's. The book was so popular it won the 1940 Pulitzer Prize. Long before the time of Steinbeck, there was another drama happening in the Middle East which could also be termed, "the grapes of wrath." It involved King Ahab, his wife Jezebel and their neighbor, Naboth. The story unfolds as Ahab asks Naboth to sell him his vineyard so he can use it for a vegetable garden. Naboth refuses for he wants to keep it for the grapes but mainly because it is his ancestral inheritance. The king becomes deeply depressed over his inability to acquire the vineyard but does not press the matter any further. Jezebel, seeing her husband so unhappy, then says that she will obtain it for him. With cunning and wrath, she has Naboth falsely accused of crime and stoned to death. Her harsh and criminal actions earned the name Jezebel eternal disrepute. Innocent victims still continue to be massacred today by wrath and greed. Yet, God's word forcefully reminds us that those who perpetrate violence on others are inviting it also upon themselves.

TUESDAY, ELEVENTH WEEK OF THE YEAR
1 K 21:17-29 and Mt 5:43-48

Although Ahab did not bring about the death of Naboth, he certainly approved of it. In today's first reading we find him out in his wickedly acquired vineyard, tearing up Naboth's ancestral vines and preparing to plant his vegetable garden. What he didn't expect to find in the vineyard was the Prophet Elijah, who proceeded to thoroughly denounce the king. Following his condemnation by Elijah, Ahab repented in the traditional manner of tearing his garments, then donning sackcloth and fasting. Through these acts of devotion, he manifests his continuing belief in his ancient Jewish traditions. Because he is repentant, God extends mercy to him. It is also implied that, because of his repentance, God would not demand his death. Jezebel, a Phoenician, did not share the religious faith of her husband and Naboth and, therefore, she easily violated these traditions which were sacred to the Israelite people. Later, Jesus would re-emphasize the power of repentance. Jezebel would not fare well for she showed no signs of regretting the evil she had done. In our day the same law continues. Many evil deeds are executed but one sincere, "I'm very sorry," can still undo much of the evil both in the eyes of God and of those who have been offended.

WEDNESDAY, ELEVENTH WEEK OF THE YEAR
2 K 2:1, 6-14 and Mt 6:1-6, 16-18

Here, we have one of the most exciting stories of the Old Testament. Elijah is taken up to heaven in a fiery chariot. He becomes like Enoch, the father of Methuselah (Gn 5:24), who ". . . walked with God, and he was no longer here, for God took him." Jewish tradition always expected Elijah to return either in person or in spirit through some other person, since it was presumed he never died. The evangelist Mark says that the people thought John the Baptizer was Elijah (Mk 6:15). And, in another place, he indicates that some were sure that Jesus was Elijah who had returned to earth (Mk 8:28). There is a pious custom among the Jewish people even to this day. When they have a party or religious celebration, they set an extra plate and chair for Elijah in anticipation of the day he will return in his horse-drawn flaming chariot. Some modern writers of science fiction see in this Prophet's fiery chariot a biblical reference to the existence of ancient spaceships. Elijah appeared to Jesus along with Moses at the Transfiguration. What really happened to Elijah, we don't know, but his spirit certainly lives on.

THURSDAY, ELEVENTH WEEK OF THE YEAR
Si 48:1-14 and Mt 6:7-15

Sirach here sings the praises of Elijah. Although Elijah lived about 850 B.C., which was probably over 600 years before Sirach was born, his reputation for marvelous deeds remained alive and very popular at the time. The name Elijah means "my God is Yahweh." He must have led a very eventful life but there is common agreement among scholars that many of the Elijah stories are legend. Some of his alleged feats were: predicting a three-year drought, being fed by the ravens, multiplying food miraculously, and raising a young man from the dead. Elijah also staged a dramatic showdown with the false prophets on Mt. Carmel. He insisted on the unique divinity of Yahweh who, in turn, faithfully supported Elijah by consuming his sacrifice with a bolt of lightning. He found God especially in the peacefulness of a gentle breeze. The name Elijah is listed in everyone's "Who's Who" in the history of religion. Among the prophets, he is chairman of the board. Sirach says no one could intimidate Elijah. What convictions do we hold today from which we can not be intimidated?

FRIDAY, ELEVENTH WEEK OF THE YEAR
2 K 11:1-4, 9-18, 20 and Mt 6:19-23

Some years ago a news commentator related the story of a major fire on the third floor of an apartment building. The fire department arrived quickly and extended a ladder to a window where a woman, with a baby in her arms, was screaming for help. Immediately, a safety net was assembled and she was told to let the child drop into the net. The child fell into the net unharmed. "Now you come down the ladder," the fire fighters called to her. Instead, she began struggling to pull a bulky mattress through the window. Holding the mattress with one hand she precariously descended the ladder, refusing to let it fall. No one understood how seemingly unconcerned she was about allowing her baby fall into the net but not the mattress. Later they were informed that she kept all her money hidden in the mattress. Our sense of values is often very clearly revealed in a crisis situation when we are pressured into letting go of some things and hanging on to others. The word, treasure, is mentioned three times in this Gospel. We can identify our true treasure by observing what it is that our heart really clings to.

SATURDAY, ELEVENTH WEEK OF THE YEAR
2 Ch 24:17-25 and Mt 6:24-34

A few years before his death, Bishop Sheen had open-heart surgery. He was clearly informed about the risk involved because of his advanced age. The surgery proceeded and, though he nearly lost his life and required an extraordinary number of blood transfusions, he recovered in an amazingly short time, again displaying his customary charm and stamina. Sometime later a reporter asked if he had been anxious about the serious heart operation or afraid of dying. The bishop said he never really had worried about dying, "for if I should leave this world," he said, "I will be in heaven with Christ and if I remain, Christ will be here with me." Jesus makes a series of statements in today's Gospel which also encourage us to worry less and trust more. The reasoning is that Our Heavenly Father made us, he knows our needs, and he will provide for our future. We may not have the nicest clothes, the biggest houses, the best food or even the longest earthly lives, but abiding faith in God will sustain us. Jesus says the secret is to simplify our lives and have fewer wants, like the birds and flowers. Then we can enjoy more what we possess and not constantly be worried about the things that we don't have.

MONDAY, TWELFTH WEEK OF THE YEAR
2 K 17:5-8, 13-15, 18 and Mt 7:1-5

How easy it is to find fault with other people. We might consider them as low-class, stupid, sinful, totally unethical or even savage. By contrast, we imagine none of these detestable characteristics as belonging to us. The original inhabitants of what is now the United States of America are often terribly maligned or ignored by many. The old western movies have done them a continuing injustice. There they were generally depicted as savages deserving to be killed. The fact is they were acting very normally, trying only to protect their lives, land and ancestral traditions. A famous Indian prayer says: "O great Spirit, whose voice I hear in the winds and whose breath gives life to all the world, hear me! I am small and weak; I need your strength and wisdom. Make my hands respect the things you have made and my ears sharp to hear your voice. Let me learn the lessons you have hidden in every leaf and rock. I seek strength, not to be greater than my brother but to fight my greatest enemy — myself. When my life fades as the sunset, may my spirit come to you without shame." Jesus told us that before we "correct" others, we must first correct ourselves.

TUESDAY, TWELFTH WEEK OF THE YEAR
2 K 19:9-11, 14-21, 31-35, 36 and Mt 7:6, 12-14

The Old Testament records many battles. The one from today's first reading has been immortalized in the famous poem of Lord Byron, "The Destruction of Sennacherib." The entire poem is too long to quote, but a few lines serve as commentary for today. "The Assyrian came down like the wolf on the fold, And his cohorts were gleaming in purple and gold; And the sheen of their spears was like stars on the sea, When the blue wave rolls nightly on deep Galilee. Like the leaves of the forest when Summer is green, That host with their banners at sunset were seen: Like the leaves of the forest when Autumn hath blown, That host on the morrow lay withered and strown." The poet, in the next three stanzas, records that the "Angel of Death" defeated the Assyrians and spared the Hebrew people. The once proud steeds and military riders of Assyria were conquered. The sixth and concluding stanza tells how the Assyrian women, back home in Ashur, cry, for the false god, Baal, did not save the Assyrian army. "And the widows of Ashur are loud in their wail, And the idols are broken in the temple of Baal; And the might of the Gentile, unsmote by the sword, Hath melted like snow in the glance of the Lord!"

WEDNESDAY, TWELFTH WEEK OF THE YEAR
2 K 22:8-13; 23:1-3 and Mt 7:15-20

Jesus said, "You can tell a tree by its fruit." If you are looking at a fruit tree and are unable to identify it; wait until the fruit appears, then you will know for sure. The appearance of fruit not only identifies the tree but tells one how productive it is. A peach tree, for example, may be strong and healthy looking, and you might think it will produce more fruit than another which may appear inferior. The real results, however, will be in the fruit, not in the appearance. Jesus tells us that the same principle is at work in human beings. It's not the person who makes a nice appearance, talks cleverly or promises much that counts, but the one who produces results. The fruit is external and observable. That will be the proof. This same test could also be helpful for ourselves, for we can be confused about our own true qualities. What really do I accomplish? Do I talk more about being busy than really being busy? It's an external world of appearance in which we live, all of which will fade away. The real is within. That makes us what and who we are. Good works come from within the sincere and loving human heart.

THURSDAY, TWELFTH WEEK OF THE YEAR
2 K 24:8-17 and Mt 7:21-29

Picture a group of us about to see God. We're filled with excitement and joy, expecting to hear all about how good we are. Finally, there we are and God says, "I don't know you." Imagine the terrible shock, pain and despair which would come with that announcement. The person in this story of Matthew is really floored when he receives that exact news. He protests that God must know him for he even worked miracles in the name of Jesus. The Lord repeats, however, that he doesn't know him. Perhaps this is meant more in the sense that God does not approve of him. Nonetheless, the person is asked to leave and is even called "an evildoer." People who are close, longtime friends endure many hardships as well as happy times together. They share their lives, discuss their plans and depend on each other. That relationship is totally different from the relationship we have with those who are casual acquaintances. Could we not say that God will know us to the degree that we share our lives, time, fears and hopes with him. Otherwise, we might be deceiving ourselves into thinking we are better friends than we really are. Can I say for sure that God and I are close friends?

FRIDAY, TWELFTH WEEK OF THE YEAR
2 K 25:1-12 and Mt 8:1-4

When the disease of leprosy was prevalent, most people would not dare get near a leper. They would certainly never touch one. That was a sure way to invite the disease into your own body. Jesus in this Gospel not only approached a leprous man but actually reached out and touched him. The Lord had worked many cures where he did not touch the person. The physical contact was not necessary in order for the cure to happen. Even so, Jesus very calmly lays his hand on this sick and disfigured soul. On the cross Jesus stretched out his hands as widely as possible and spiritually embraced all us "lepers" who were afflicted with the disease of sin. The Lord was the pure and innocent Savior, who was unafraid to touch any contaminated victims who were suffering from physical or spiritual diseases.

We have all been touched by God's loving mercy even though we may not have felt it. Touching another can be mutually healing, for we all need the human support that we alone can give to one another. Remaining aloof is like saying we don't accept you entirely. The sacraments of the Church all involve a personal contact. We cannot count all the ways God comes to us through the human touch.

SATURDAY, TWELFTH WEEK OF THE YEAR
Lm 2:2, 10-14, 18-19 and Mt 8:5-17

The Book of Lamentations consists of five chapters. Each is a poem written in the form of a dirge. The subject matter pertains to the fall of Jerusalem in 587 B.C. at the hands of the Babylonians. This passage from the second poem says that Israel was conquered and taken into exile because of its unfaithfulness to God. The reason the people are facing this terrible suffering in captivity is that Israel's prophets did not fulfill their proper roles. They were not forthright in the messages they preached to the people and to that extent, they did not do what they had to do as prophets. The text tells us explicitly: "Your prophets had for you false and specious visions. They did not lay bare your guilt to avert your fate." The Hebrew Prophets were expected to make their stern pronouncements, like today's umpires: "Call 'em and walk away." You can't be concerned if you call out the league's leading hitter or if it's your nephew at bat. Whatever the pitch, it must be called as it is. The prophets, therefore, were expected to always speak the blunt and naked truth, and then let the chips fall where they may.

MONDAY, THIRTEENTH WEEK OF THE YEAR
Am 2:6-10, 13-16 and Mt 8:18-22

If an employer would refuse to release an employee from a day's work to attend his or her father's funeral, we would judge that employer to be about the most heartless person imaginable. We might get the impression Jesus is demanding something unreasonable of those who are and wish to become his followers. To the disciple who wanted to go and bury his father, Jesus says, "Follow me, and let the dead bury their dead." We know Jesus was not heartless with people and especially when they were in the midst of sorrow. The Lord is not forbidding a person to attend his father's funeral. When this disciple states he wants to bury his father before he comes to follow Jesus, the implication is that his father is still alive and may be years from death. He wants to care for his father and mother and assist them with their business affairs. Then after they have died and matters are settled, he'll come and be a disciple. Jesus is saying the disciple should not wait until his parents die. Follow now. Part of being a disciple is to respond immediately, trusting that other matters will be provided for.

TUESDAY, THIRTEENTH WEEK OF THE YEAR
Am 3:1-8; 4:11-12 and Mt 8:23-27

We know from our studies and from daily observation that there is a cause for every effect. The apparent cause may not be the true one but, nonetheless, there is some cause for every happening. In this passage the prophet Amos reminds the Hebrew people that many wonderful things have happened to them. They are now simply taking those beautiful blessings for granted and not showing appreciation to God, who is the one who caused them. He presents his case in a series of questions which all imply a negative answer. Does a lion roar and people remain unafraid? No, the roaring lion scares people. Do you find two people walking together, unless they have agreed to? No, somewhere or sometime they had to decide to be friends. Can the warm days of spring come, we might ask, without flowers and grass also appearing? No, the season invites the flowers to appear and display their lovely colors. Can we be born, breathe, and live peaceful lives without the intervention of God? No, God is the cause of all that exists and we, human beings, are part of the effects.

WEDNESDAY, THIRTEENTH WEEK OF THE YEAR
Am 5:14-15, 21-24 and Mt 8:28-34

Swine are held in very low esteem in the Middle East. They are unfairly discriminated against and mercilessly condemned simply for being what, by nature, they are meant to be. A flock of sheep is said to have dignity and is held in respect. Herds of swine by contrast are regarded as unclean and unworthy of respect. Jesus caters to these strong feelings of the people as he dispossesses two men of evil spirits. The presumption is that demons must inhabit someone or something — they can not simply roam at large. In a type of bargaining, Jesus agrees to free the two men at the expense of — you guessed it — the swine. Frightened, the whole herd rushed over the cliff and were drowned. Even pig lovers can accept the symbolic lesson. We are to be possessed by the Holy Spirit, not the spirit of evil. Jesus frees us from those sins and spirits which can dominate our lives and lead us to death. The two men, formerly living under the influence of evil, are now set free to live a self-possessed human life. Jesus came to destroy those things which torture us.

THURSDAY, THIRTEENTH WEEK OF THE YEAR
Am 7:10-17 and Mt 9:1-8

To be paralyzed means to be unable to move a part of the body. It is truly pitiful to see a person who has had a stroke and is left with paralyzed limbs. The hand and arm, meant to lift objects, now become heavy objects themselves. They can move only if they are lifted by the other hand and arm. Jesus, here, encounters a paralyzed man. The Lord seems to ignore his paralysis and sees him only as a spiritual person. Therefore, he forgives his sins. Knowing his action would generate controversy, Jesus was prepared for his next move. Forgiveness of sins is internal and unseen and, therefore, difficult to demonstrate. Curing the body is observable and easily verifiable. The cure of the body was a clear testimony to the healing of the soul. We may have suffered a spiritual paralysis somewhere along the way. Perhaps, it brought our inner lives of faith and love to a grinding halt. Now, everything spiritual is heavy and death-like in appearance. We can't move and be moved by the Spirit as we used to. Take courage, have heart, says Jesus. You, too, can stand up again and walk. When freed from sin and cured within, who knows what marvelous other results may follow.

FRIDAY, THIRTEENTH WEEK OF THE YEAR
Am 8:4-6, 9-12 and Mt 9:9-13

Three impressive qualities of Jesus are highlighted in this Gospel. (1) Jesus was an activist. He moved about freely in all types of company. Openly, he called people to abandon their dissipated way of life and follow him. There was nothing reclusive about the Lord; rather, he was characterized by his energetic and outgoing daily schedule. (2) Jesus was a teacher. That was his reputation and people respected him in that role. They openly called him teacher. The Lord enlightened minds and taught earthly as well as eternal truths. The New Testament simply overflows with the wisdom of Jesus. (3) Jesus was a doctor. He had the calling of a divine physician and often referred to himself as such. He made various comparisons to the medical sciences and his cures were frequent, dramatic and enduring. Armed with such wonderful assets, Jesus was more than a match for any rival, especially, the upstart. In this Gospel passage we view Jesus functioning skillfully in these capacities. We can think of and pray to Jesus under these images. Invite the divine activist, knowledgeable teacher, and skillful doctor to direct your lives.

SATURDAY, THIRTEENTH WEEK OF THE YEAR
Am 9:11-15 and Mt 9:14-17

In his message to Congress, January 6, 1941, President Franklin D. Roosevelt said he wanted to "make secure" the future. He would do this by fashioning a better world based on his famous four freedoms. He listed them as: (1) Freedom of speech and expression, (2) Freedom to worship God in your own way, (3) Freedom from want, and, finally, (4) Freedom from fear . . . anywhere in the world. In this speech the President was re-echoing the Constitution of the United States which is a reflection of the teachings of Sacred Scripture. The Old and New Testaments are both filled with hopeful thoughts and dreams of a better future. This passage from the prophet Amos comprises the last verses of the last chapter of his book. It's his hope that the Hebrews will reform and the future will be joyful. He forecasts a time of stability during which they can eat the fruit of their gardens and drink the wine of the vineyards they have planted. Happiness is finding security in this world and a realistic hope of future, spiritual security in the next.

MONDAY, FOURTEENTH WEEK OF THE YEAR
Ho 2:16, 17-18, 21-22 and Mt 9:18-26

The marriage covenant is often used in Scripture as a symbol of God's relationship with his chosen people. This particular passage in Hosea is one of the classic texts on the subject of love, unfaithfulness, and repeated forgiveness. If Hosea and Gomer would have known before hand what lay ahead in their marriage, they might have cancelled the event at the wedding rehearsal. The story, written from Hosea's point of view, says he loved her dearly and did everything possible to be a faithful husband. Gomer is pictured as being very restless and wanting to be with other men. The story is well known. It tells that Hosea continually seeks, finds, and brings her back home. This passage today shows how close the people were to God during their time in Egypt and then in the forty years in the desert. The Lord, speaking as a husband, wants to entice his people back to that desert-relationship. We are the ones God is calling today. The invitation is to return to that love and trusting friendship with God which we used to have.

TUESDAY, FOURTEENTH WEEK OF THE YEAR
Ho 8:4-7, 11-13 and Mt 9:32-38

Jesus related to individual people in an excellent manner. He was free, easy going, and friendly. He also had the unique ability of relating to the crowds which he encountered. This crowd moved his heart to have pity on them. I must not think of Jesus as existing only for me. He is my shepherd but he is also the shepherd of all others. I am only part of the crowd. The ratio is not one shepherd for one sheep, but one shepherd for all sheep. It would be a good and correct Christian way of thinking if we would always consider ourselves as part of the crowd. Maybe we've been told not to be part of the crowd but to stand alone. That's good advice in one way and not so good in another. When we have a crowd-mentality, we think as a member of a community. We move as a group, being highly dependent on each other. If I can improve myself, I automatically make the community a better place. Jesus sees the crowd present here in church with our hopes and hurts. Be our shepherd, Lord, and lead us to salvation.

WEDNESDAY, FOURTEENTH WEEK OF THE YEAR
Ho 10:1-3, 7-8, 12 and Mt 10:1-7

The word apostle means one who is sent on a mission. Jesus is an apostle sent from God. In one Scripture verse (Heb 3:1), he is called precisely that. From the One sent from God, others are sent from him and by him, out into the world. In the New Testament the term refers primarily to the Twelve Apostles. A contemporary analogy might be that of a football team. The seventy two disciples were all the members on the squad, and twelve from these were hand picked to be the starting team. They were personally chosen by Jesus after observation and a night of private prayer. Each had unique assets for the ministry which would be required of them. Some were a bit more privileged, namely Peter, James and John. They shared intimately in both the delight of the Lord's transfiguration on the mountain and in the deep agony of his prayer in the garden. They were privileged to hear the private words and thoughts of Jesus, which the others did not. They were sent on a mission to tell of the birth, life, death and resurrection of Jesus and most, if not all, lost their lives in the process. In fact, we possess our faith today because these first apostles accomplished their mission so well.

THURSDAY, FOURTEENTH WEEK OF THE YEAR
Ho 11:1, 3-4, 8-9 and Mt 10:7-15

These instructions to the first apostles give strong evidence that Jesus expected them to have tremendous faith. Not only were they to base their future lives on faith but their day-to-day physical existence also depended on it. In the travel section of some bookstores, you often see titles like "How to Tour Europe On $5.00 a Day." It surely sounds like an inexpensive way to travel. Jesus programmed an even less expensive way. He told his apostles to travel with no budget for expenses and no material security at all. They were to take absolutely no money. It's spelled out even more definitely: ". . . neither gold, nor silver, nor copper in your belts." Likewise, they were to have no change of clothing, no sandals and no walking stick to lean on or use for self defense. They were even to shake the dust from their feet and leave even that behind if the people did not accept them. The apostles were to be as the flowers of the field and the birds of the air which are completely provided for by the Heavenly Father. Faith says that the more we give the more we get in return. I wonder how I would fare if my total livelihood depended on the strength of my faith.

FRIDAY, FOURTEENTH WEEK OF THE YEAR
Ho 14:2-10 and Mt 10:16-23

Hosea, like Amos, concludes the last chapter of his book on a hopeful note. He calls for Israel to return to the Lord in faithful trust. The passage reads like a penitential ceremony. The people are to confess that they cannot be saved through foreign powers like Assyria, nor by false gods which are the works of their own hands. God promises to be "like dew for Israel." That is a symbol of newness and fresh beginning, for the dew appears at the dawning of a new day. The dew also gives moisture to the arid land, causing the vegetation to grow. We can easily see from the imagery that the author lives in a hot, dry climate, for blessings come in the form of blossoms, flowers, dew and shade. The whole tone of this passage is to return to what you once were. Jesus would later teach the same message when he called for adults to become again like little children. To be holy then doesn't mean we should become something new and different. It simply means to be now what we once were in the most innocent years of our lives. Give some thought today to how you might think, talk or act now with the same innocence you had as a child.

SATURDAY, FOURTEENTH WEEK OF THE YEAR
Is 6:1-8 and Mt 10:24-33

This passage from the prophet Isaiah is a very well known and much used text of Scripture. In it Isaiah tells of a vision he had of God in the temple, during which he is called to his sacred mission of ministry. We note the "Holy, holy, holy . . . Lord of hosts," which we all recognize from its use in the Preface of the Mass. The Hebrew language did not have the comparative and superlative forms of the adjective, only the positive. To express the superlative, the positive had to be repeated three times. In English we could easily say "most holy," but the triple positive is retained to give us a sense of tradition. When we sing the Sanctus, remember we are recalling Isaiah's vision. We, too, can picture God's most holy throne on high surrounded by those most distinguished angels, the Seraphim, hovering aloft. The vision can make us sense our need to purify our hearts and lips as we prepare to receive the sacred bread and wine of the Eucharist. The experience can also inspire us to seek the purgation of our sins, so that we may be made worth of our calling as Isaiah was. The famous text also invites us to renew our own sense of mission. "Here I am, Lord" standing ready. "Send me" on my mission of love this day.

MONDAY, FIFTEENTH WEEK OF THE YEAR
Is 1:10-17 and Mt 10:34 - 11:1

Jesus is often thought of as the world's most outstanding peacemaker. Here the Lord is quoted as saying, "My mission is to spread, not peace, but division." When he was presented in the temple as a six-week-old baby, Simeon had said the child would cause some to fall and some to rise and that he would be a sign of opposition. As a mature adult, Jesus now reaffirms Simeon's prediction. Here the Lord says that because of him there will be divisions within one's immediate family and among the in-laws. In our attempt to please God, we may displease others. That may cause division. Think of those people who are extremely close to you in friendship. Jesus says that he, too, expects to be part of that close immediate friendship. When we prefer other people to the Lord, we are not worthy of the Lord. When we choose to be honest to God, at the expense of straining a human friendship, then we are making a true Christian commitment and carrying our cross. The principle of having "peace at all cost" is not scripturally valid. Being honest to God is the basis of true Christian morality and must be given preference.

TUESDAY, FIFTEENTH WEEK OF THE YEAR
Is 7:1-9 and Mt 11:20-24

This is the "Farewell to Galilee" talk. Jesus is disappointed because the towns where he preached most reformed very poorly. Bethsaida is on the unfavorable list. It was a fishing village on the northern shore of the Sea of Galilee, frequented by at least three of the apostles: Peter, Andrew and Philip. A blind man was healed by Jesus there, and nearby the loaves were multiplied. The faith of the people in that place should have been stronger. Like its sister village of Chorazin, it is lost to history. Capernaum, the home of Peter and Andrew, was the site of most of our Lord's miracles. He did some of his most important preaching there. But it did not live up to Jesus' expectations. Tyre and Sidon, by contrast, were Gentile cities. They had witnessed no recorded miracles by Jesus. Nor had they heard him preach. Judgment would be easier on them. Sodom had been considered the epitome of wickedness and had already been destroyed. We, today, are like the people of Chorazin, Bethsaida and Capernaum. We have heard the preaching, seen the miracles and eaten the miraculous loaves. Jesus, therefore, expects us to be among his most loyal believers. If we were primitive pagans we would not be expected to have deep faith but, in reality, a tremendous amount of preaching and teaching has been invested in us. Much more, therefore, is required of us, since so much more has been given.

WEDNESDAY, FIFTEENTH WEEK OF THE YEAR
Is 10:5-7, 13-16 and Mt 11:25-27

Family members, who are loving and open with each other, form a strong bond of deep understanding. Jesus uses that precious association of the caring father and loving son to describe his own relationship with his Father. Jesus promises that we, too, can have a loving relationship with God as he does. The reason is that Jesus has made us God's adopted sons and daughters. A few years ago, there was a true story on TV about a baron in Germany who owned a 130-room castle overlooking the Rhine River. He wanted it to remain in the family name but he had no heirs. The baron, therefore, advertised for some adult who was willing to be adopted into his family. A husband and wife from Michigan were selected. Their names were changed to that of the baron and they inherited the castle and grounds. They were expected to move to Germany, be caretakers of the castle, and keep it in the family name. It was given to them free of charge. God is our Father and we are all adopted through the life and deeds of Jesus, our brother. We are to be caretakers of what we possess and take pride in our new name of Christian. Thus it is promised we will inherit the kingdom.

THURSDAY, FIFTEENTH WEEK OF THE YEAR
Is 26:7-9, 12, 16-19 and Mt 11:28-30

One of the little "charmers" by Hallmark, caught my attention some time ago, so I clipped it from the newspaper and taped it to the wall. It pictures a small boy beside his bicycle, holding a tire pump. The front tire is flat. His Scottish Terrier is beside him trying to be helpful. The caption reads: "Problems are challenges in disguise." When ordinary problems come each day we could feel very burdened, even overwhelmed. We might throw up our hands in disgust. We could also lift our hands in a prayer of thanksgiving for the little disciplines of life. Our scriptural reading today is very brief but one that is applied in many circumstances. It is simply a lovely little Gospel passage. Here is contained a personal promise from the Lord. The key thought is, burdens become lighter when humanly and divinely shared. No doubt we could all use a better theology about coping with daily problems. They are part of every day's agenda and to be expected. No one likes problems but most people do like challenges. We make our problems lighter both by renaming them and seeing God's hand lifting them, as is promised in today's Gospel.

FRIDAY, FIFTEENTH WEEK OF THE YEAR
Is 38:1-6, 21-22, 7-8 and Mt 12:1-8

Jesus and his apostles "break" the Sabbath law which forbids them to work on that day. The physical labor involved in pulling and shelling a few heads of wheat is hardly called work, but it was classified as such by the Pharisees. There were thirty nine forms of work which were forbidden on the Sabbath and preparing food was one of them. In this situation Jesus had an answer, as he always did. He says that King David and his men, in their need, did what was forbidden on the Sabbath. They ate the holy bread which was forbidden to anyone except the priests. Indirectly, Jesus is saying that he, too, is a king — David's equal and more. The Lord then adds that priests are permitted to break the Sabbath work law without incurring any guilt. Indirectly, he is stating that he is a priest and more. Jesus and his followers are, therefore, not breaking the law. The Pharisees should show more respect to Jesus and acknowledge his unique dignity because, in him, they have something greater than the temple. Jesus is in full compliance with the commandment which says: "Remember, keep holy the Sabbath." As Son of God and Messiah, Jesus is asking the Pharisees to accept and honor him at least as much as they honor the Sabbath.

SATURDAY, FIFTEENTH WEEK OF THE YEAR
Mi 2:1-5 and Mt 12:14-21

Matthew is famous for returning to the Hebrew Scriptures and there finding texts which fulfill the mission of Jesus. Many of these quotations are in his infancy account where he quotes Isaiah, Micah and Jeremiah. His favorite source is Isaiah. Matthew's reading public was mainly Jewish. They would be well versed in the Old Testament readings and no doubt impressed to learn that Jesus was the individual to whom these texts make reference. If Matthew could show how Jesus fulfilled the words of the prophets, then the people could more easily accept Jesus as the Messiah. Here, again, Matthew turns to quoting Isaiah. It is a wonderful statement regarding the Lord's kind sensitivity. We may be holding on to life with a thread, as a single strand holding together two pieces of palm, and the Lord will not tear us loose. We may be flickering, about to burn out, as a candle in a wind storm, and the Lord will still help us preserve our tiny spark of life, no matter how insignificant. All who are Gentiles especially rejoice, for here it is stated that in the Lord the Gentiles will find hope. Is this prophecy fulfilled in our lives?

MONDAY, SIXTEENTH WEEK OF THE YEAR
Mi 6:1-4, 6-8 and Mt 12:38-42

The Prophet Micah says: "Do what is right, love what is good and walk humbly with your God." He is also the author of another wonderful statement which has been quoted by Matthew and read in the churches throughout the world on the Feast of the Epiphany. "And you, Bethlehem, land of Judah, are by no means least among the princes of Judah, since from you shall come a ruler who is to shepherd my people Israel." The seven chapters in the book of Micah are a series of threats and promises. They cover the entire gamut of social ills. Woes are directed against the rich, the rulers, and the false prophets. The major threat he uses to demand a national reform is the destruction of the country by a foreign power. His promises include help for the poor, the conquering of their national enemies, and the future protection of Yahweh. In the passage we read today, Micah is pleading with the people to be appreciative to their God for all the blessings they have received in the past. The last verse of this section tells us what to do, viz., the right, what to love, viz., the good, and how to walk, viz., humbly with our God. It's a fine guide for daily living.

TUESDAY, SIXTEENTH WEEK OF THE YEAR
Mi 7:14-15, 18-20 and Mt 12:46-50

This Scripture passage is a real morale booster for those who might feel like the nobodies of the world. In essence its message is, "You don't need to have an impressive title, lots of wealth or be related to someone who does." In the eyes of the Lord it's not who you are but what you are that counts. Jesus shows no favoritism, even to his earthly family. His mother and some "brothers" apparently wanted him to stop speaking to the common crowd and come outside to speak to them about some undisclosed matter. When told of their request, Jesus in a very nice but very pointed way said that his mother, father, brothers and sisters were right here, in the people of the crowd. Isn't it encouraging to realize that the Son of God considers the common people of the world as close to him as a mother or brother or sister would be? The only qualification for the Lord to see us on that level of intimacy is that we do the will of our heavenly Father. In the Our Father we pray, "Thy will be done." That means, may God's will be done, not only in some abstract manner, but by me — personally and faithfully each day. That makes me an intimate member of God's family.

WEDNESDAY, SIXTEENTH WEEK OF THE YEAR
Jr 1:1, 4-10 and Mt 13:1-9

Jeremiah was expected to preach, but he was afraid and thought only of the reasons why he could not or should not. He told God he couldn't talk for he was too young and inexperienced. We can be very much like Jeremiah — overly conscious of the many things we are unable to do, or at least think we can't. God assured Jeremiah he was fully capable of the task to which he was called. "The will of God will place you only where the grace of God will keep you." That modern day saying can give us courage when we start to get the "Jeremiah blues." It seems the prophet did not have a very happy life and never did like his calling. It's possible he could have been more contented and productive had he been able to express a more positive attitude. Our attitudes are vital. A negative outlook is the quickest way to defeat ourselves, for even if we have no major problems our attitude produces them. If we believe we can do all things in the Lord who strengthens us, chances are we will.

THURSDAY, SIXTEENTH WEEK OF THE YEAR
Jr 2:1-3, 7-8, 12-13 and Mt 13:10-17

Why did Jesus teach so many profound truths in parables? The apostles asked this question and we, too, might like to know. Many would reject the teachings of Jesus if he spoke of the mysteries of God in a way with which they were not familiar. They would simply judge he was not telling the truth because the truth would be difficult to prove. By using parables, Jesus reasoned that his skeptical hearers would be more inclined to accept at least some truth of the story, the part which they might understand. They would not get all the implications of the message but neither would they reject it totally. A parable seemed the best medium of communication to make at least some progress. A parable also is open to various interpretations. Since we often hear truths in accordance with what is happening inside of us, each could apply the parable as personally needed. Many longed to hear the words of the Messiah, but they never heard them. Those who heard were blessed. We are even more blessed to have heard the words of salvation passed on to us through twenty centuries of practical Christian living.

FRIDAY, SIXTEENTH WEEK OF THE YEAR
Jr 3:14-17 and Mt 13:18-23

Four different times in this Gospel it is implied that a seed is like a person. The presumption is that seeds are similar but they produce different results because of the various types of ground where they grow. People, like seeds, are probably more alike than we might think. The circumstances of our lives and the different environments where we live create many types and styles of life. Whether we live along the path, on the rocks, in the briers or within the good soil, remember, we are seeds. As a seed, I originated from another seed and that seed from a previous one. The first seed came from God. Since I am a seed, I am meant to do what every seed does — grow. Every seed has a long-range future goal to produce something. Maybe apples, peaches, lumber, shade, etc. What am I attempting to produce? Within me there is contained all the history of the past and all the hope of the future. We need to be in tune with the seasons of life and each year move closer to our goal. The Gospel says we should reach for the good ground of God's grace, nourishment and sunshine. Only when well grounded in divine love, can we become all we are meant to be.

SATURDAY, SIXTEENTH WEEK OF THE YEAR
Jr 7:1-11 and Mt 13:24-30

Jeremiah is told to stand at the door of the temple and be a greeter to those who are entering to worship. He is to speak very differently than the ordinary greeter at the church door today. His message is not, "Hello, Mr. and Mrs. Smith. My, how nice you look today. How's your daughter in Cincinnati?" No, Jeremiah is more confrontational and challenging. He reminds all on the way in that they are to be very serious about their prayers and open to hear the word of the Lord. "Don't just drift in to occupy a seat simply because you are expected to be present. Come here only to pray, for this is the temple of the Lord." Imagine a modern day greeter standing at the entrance shouting to the people to reform their lives, deal justly with their neighbor, not to oppress the alien or take advantage of the widow or orphan. "You can't continue to murder, steal, commit adultery and lie and still come and stand in church. Don't come here thinking you're safe because you are present. This house bears God's name. We don't want it to become a den of thieves." Later, Jesus would echo these same words before he, too, cleansed the temple.

MONDAY, SEVENTEENTH WEEK OF THE YEAR
Jr 13:1-11 and Mt 13:31-35

It is the nature of the mustard seed to grow, branch out and welcome the birds of the world. It is the nature of yeast to rise up, expand and turn the waiting dough into bread for the hungry of the world. It was of the nature of Jesus to begin as a tiny baby, like a mustard seed. It was of his nature to expand as the yeast into the bread of life, for those in need of food. The outdoor parable of the seed and the indoor one of the dough, show the two dimensions of Christian development. Membership is to expand in numbers and countries of the world. The members, likewise, are called to develop within, so the Church is always expanding both in quantity and quality. As we ponder the various parables of Jesus we can continue to discover their meanings in our individual lives. The Lord said these are teachings and they are to announce truths which have long been hidden. We can make a personal application of these two parables by looking out and looking within. How broad are my vistas? How deep are my commitments?

TUESDAY, SEVENTEENTH WEEK OF THE YEAR
Jr 14:17-22 and Mt 13:35-43

Sometimes the future looks bleak, as stated in this newspaper article. "It's a gloomy moment in the history of our country.
Not in the lifetime of most men has there been so much grave and
deep apprehension. Never has the future seemed so dismal. The
domestic economic situation is in chaos. Our dollar is weak
throughout the world. Prices are so high as to be utterly impossible. The political cauldron seethes and bubbles with un-
certainties. It's a solemn, solemn moment of our troubles. No
man can see the end." This quotation is an editorial from the
Boston Herald American, written in 1857. The readers at that
time must have viewed their future with a sense of hopelessness
bordering on panic. Jeremiah had the same dismal outlook for
Israel in the seventh century B.C. Today's reading is a poem
lamenting the fate of his country, personified as a young woman
mortally wounded. The picture is not a pretty one. It is painted
with tears, sleepless nights and destruction. There are scenes of
the slain, the starving and the depressed. Yet, there is still hope
in God, based on the covenant. And so a prayer is offered for
better days. Hope remains stronger than despair. Annie still
sings, "I love you, tomorrow . . . The sun will come out tomorrow, bet your bottom dollar."

WEDNESDAY, SEVENTEENTH WEEK OF THE YEAR
Jr 15:10, 16-21 and Mt 13:44-46

This Gospel takes us on a treasure hunt. One treasure is
found buried in a field and a valuable pearl is buried in the water.
The finders, having discovered them, will go to any length or cost
to obtain permanent possession. Treasures make us think of
things like money, jewels, precious metals or a whole collection of

mysterious objects of fantastic values. If you have a thesaurus on
your book shelf, you have a treasure. The Latin word for treasure
is thesaurus. It contains a wealth of words which we can easily
find and freely use. Our friends are treasures, for life would be
terrible without them. Anything of outstanding value must in
some way qualify as a treasure. Jesus spoke of treasures here
because he wanted us to know that "the reign of God is like a
buried treasure." We do not earn the kingdom, it is something we
find in Jesus. In baptism we found a pearl of deep value. In our
hearts we find faith, hope, love and grace. Because of the gifts of
Jesus we are so rich in treasures, we can't even appreciate how
much we are worth.

THURSDAY, SEVENTEENTH WEEK OF THE YEAR
Jr 18:1-6 and Mt 13:47-53R

The modern religious song entitled, "Abba! Father," which
is composed by Carey Landry, bases part of its refrain on
Jeremiah 18:6. This passage of Scripture is read as the first
lesson of today's liturgy. The flowing melody and beautiful
meditative lyrics convey the thoughts of God being Father and
potter, while we are the clay. We are molded and fashioned by
God's hands into the image of Jesus. The song concludes by
giving glory and praise to God for ordering the existence to our
lives. The whole theme of shaping clay into human life reminds
one of the Genesis creation story. The name Adam, means one
who is taken from clay, from the ground. That story revolves
around the same theme that God is the potter and we are the clay.
In the work of the potter, each vessel is shaped individually by the
hand. None are mass produced. The hand of the potter, in a
sense, leaves a unique trademark on each creation. We are
continually being shaped into a more perfect image. To be shaped
we must be pliable, willing to be pressured, squeezed and pushed

into whatever type of vessel the potter desires. See the hand of God in your life each day shaping you for the eternal future. Tomorrow we will be a bit different than we are today.

FRIDAY, SEVENTEENTH WEEK OF THE YEAR
Jr 26:1-9 and Mt 13:54-58

One summer some Midwesterners were vacationing in Maryland along the Chesapeake Bay. At the time James Michener was living in the area and working on his book, *Chesapeake.* As they were walking through the historic shipbuilding town of St. Michael's they saw posters advertising a coming social event to be held at the local hotel. It featured a dinner and discussion with James Michener. The cost was $20.00. The big attraction of course was the opportunity to meet and chat with this world famous author. As they browsed through the shops they asked one of the residents if she were going to attend the event. "Heavens no!" she replied. "Why should I pay $20.00 to see Michener? Why, I see him at the post office nearly every day." This seems to be the same mind-set the people of Nazareth had about Jesus. They could see him most anytime in their narrow, dusty streets. Especially, since he was raised in their town, he didn't appear to them to be any "big deal." Jesus said of his hometown people: "No prophet is without honor except in his native place, indeed in his own house." Regardless of how familiar we might feel with Jesus, we should never lose our reverential awe.

SATURDAY, SEVENTEENTH WEEK OF THE YEAR
Jr 26:11-16, 24 and Mt 14:1-12

Herod's fear-filled statements about Jesus and John the Baptizer in this Gospel are often overshadowed by the entrance of Salome, the dancing girl. If we would read only verses one through five and stop, we would get a unique insight into the mind of Herod. The Herod referred to here is Herod Antipas. When studying in Rome, he had met Herodias and fell in love. In order to be with her, Herod had to divorce his wife, Aretas, and Herodias had to divorce her husband, Herod Philip. Their subsequent marriage caused great public scandal among the Jews, since Herod was their governor, ruling under the direction of Rome. Inasmuch as this imperial marriage was currently an inflammatory topic, John the Baptizer publicly rebuked the offending couple. For his open condemnation of their sinful relationship, John was arrested by Herod who had him locked up in jail. Herod wanted to get rid of John but he feared an adverse reaction of the people whose cause John had championed. Later however, following Salome's dance, Herod was pressured into having John executed through the manipulation of Herodias. His viciously sinful deed must have given him nightmares. Now he sees Jesus as the reincarnation of John, for Jesus, too, is outspoken and blunt. When Pilate sent Jesus to Herod as a prisoner, Jesus refused even to speak to him. Herod wanted to kill Jesus and, thereby, "kill John," a second time. The alternative to murder would have been repentance and a change of life. For some, the cost of virtue is too high a price to pay.

MONDAY, EIGHTEENTH WEEK OF THE YEAR
Jr 28:1-17 and Mt 14:13-21

Here is a passage of Scripture that enables us to see something of the motives underlying the actions of Jesus. Matthew begins by pointing out that Jesus was saddened by the death of John, his cousin and co-worker in the ministry. He felt a pressing need within himself to retreat from what he was doing in order to spend some quiet time in prayer with his apostles. They, therefore, deliberately chose "a deserted place." The crowd, with much effort, also found the spot and came on foot to the place. It is said that Jesus "had pity on them." The word pity is from the Latin — "pietas." It means to be pious, especially by showing an almost devotional compassion to those who are suffering. Jesus extended his pity to these people in these sad circumstances because they, too, were lamenting the death of John the Baptizer. For some, John had been their spokesman and their guide. In life, he had directed our Lord's first disciples to him; now in death he sends many of his other followers to Jesus. The Lord, in his compassion, ministers to them in two ways. Some are sick so Jesus heals them. All are hungry so Jesus provides bread. When sick or hungry we can search out the pious Jesus and know we will not be sent away empty.

TUESDAY, EIGHTEENTH WEEK OF THE YEAR
Jr 30:1-2, 12-15, 18-22 and Mt 14:22-36

Jesus and his disciples had gone to a deserted place to be alone in thought and prayer, but a mass of people had assembled seeking healings and other blessings. Now the crowd had gone and he "insisted" that the disciples take the boat to the other side of the lake. Matthew tells us that Jesus remained alone in prayer "as evening drew on." Since it was not until three in the morning that he came walking on the water, Jesus must have spent at least ten hours in private communication with his Father. Notice how this mini-retreat energized him. He has apparently come to some acceptance of John's death and recommitted himself to his own increasingly dangerous mission. He walks on water — the only recorded incident of the Lord's doing that. He could have walked on water for the crowd and made a tremendous impression on them, but chose to perform this feat in the dark and for the benefit of his apostles only. He gives his chosen leader, Peter, an impressive lesson about his own unsure footing in the future and how he will need to depend on faith. When his faith weakens, he must cry out for help. Here the Lord displays the source of strength in his personal life, namely prayer. And he impressively demonstrated to the Apostles their own need for prayer if they are to survive in the future. They, in turn, have taught this lesson to us.

WEDNESDAY, EIGHTEENTH WEEK OF THE YEAR
Jr 31:1-7 and Mt 15:21-28

This passage is an exciting poem, joyfully commemorating the peoples' return from exile. Their boundless exhuberance at having their freedom again is clearly expressed in these lines. Also, present is the implicit promise on the part of the people to be more faithful to God's commandments. There is a reference here to the Exodus from Egypt under Moses. Their return from exile is seen as a new exodus. The poem emphasizes the remnant, i.e., the small group of faithful believers who never deserted God. God responds to their faithfulness with a renewal of the covenant. A powerful line in this reading comes from God, spoken to these faithful people. "With age-old love I have loved you. . . ." It's another way of saying that God's love is eternal; it always has been and always will be. Love looks both directions — to the past and to the future. The older and more intense it has been in the past, the more assurance there is of its continuance into the future. Eternal love is all-embracing. Since we profess the eternal nature of God's love, we believe that whatever was said about covenant, caring, and forgiving in the past will generously be extended to us now and to future generations.

THURSDAY, EIGHTEENTH WEEK OF THE YEAR
Jr 31:31-34 and Mt 16:13-23

The ancient Greek philosopher, Plato, is much read and quoted even today. He is especially remembered for his reflective insights into the existence of the natural law. In his effort to demonstrate it, Plato gives the example of a person confined to a dark cave from birth. Even though he had never enjoyed contact with the outside world, such a person, Plato says, would still have some notion of God's existence and a concept of right and wrong. His famous "cave example" is supposed to give credence to the theory that we know more than is taught to us by people and circumstances. There is a certain innate sense of what is and is not appropriate, common to all people, which we call the natural law. We have no evidence Plato ever read Jeremiah, but such could have been possible since he lived nearly 250 years after Jeremiah and there was commerce between the two countries. In Jeremiah's passage, read today, we note some of the characteristics of the natural law. The Prophet says there is a law in our hearts, divinely written, by which we innately know God. Regardless of our varied backgrounds and personal contacts, we have a similar basic sense of right and wrong.

FRIDAY, EIGHTEENTH WEEK OF THE YEAR
Na 2:1, 3; 3:1-3, 6-7 and Mt 16:24-28

Jesus, here, presents another of his famous paradoxes: "Whoever would save his life will lose it, but whoever will lose his life for my sake will find it." This famous quotation has literally been proved true in so many instances. Howard Hughes, for example, was determined to save his life from the invasion of germs by providing himself with an isolated, germ-free environment. In spite of all his wealth, he lost his freedom, his happiness and ultimately his sanity, dying as a mysterious and strange recluse. In contrast, Mother Theresa left her safe environment in a fashionable girls' school to go out among the dying, germ-infected people of the streets. She personally took them in her arms, brought them to a safe haven away from the gutters of Calcutta, gave them food and medicine and a clean bed so they could at least die in some dignity. She "gave her life away" and, thereby, found it. In between these extremes we live. We, too, must make our unique application of the teachings of Jesus to our own existence. Saving our lives is not nearly as beneficial as spending them.

SATURDAY, EIGHTEENTH WEEK OF THE YEAR
Hb 1:12 - 2:4 and Mt 17:14-20

Jesus tells us that if we had faith the size of a mustard seed, we could move a mountain. Imagine a tiny seed — no bigger than a rain drop — engaged in a shoving match with a gigantic mountain. If the mustard seed were made out of pure, concentrated, 100% faith, the mountain would be pushed back. It's a colorful statement and it certainly makes a powerful impact. Imagine if our faith were the size of a mountain. In that case we could move the world. It was the mountain-sized belief in the power and goodness of his heavenly Father which brought Jesus to Calvary to save the world and move the hearts of all its people. He was rewarded in the resurrection. Later in the Gospel narrative, Luke speaks of faith the size of a mustard seed. He quotes Jesus as saying that it could uproot a sycamore tree and hurl it into the sea. The apostles had such a small degree of belief that Jesus told them they were "a perverse and unbelieving race." Faith connects us directly to the one in whom we believe. Complete faith in God gives the believer fantastic power. Jesus personally explains how strong faith could change our lives: "Nothing would be impossible for you," he says.

MONDAY, NINETEENTH WEEK OF THE YEAR
Ezk 1:2-5, 24-28 and Mt 17:22-27

The four evangelists, who collected and recorded the different accounts of the Gospel, were impressed or intrigued by some stories more than others. This incident of collecting taxes for the temple is preserved only by Matthew. It was simply omitted by the other three. We would expect Matthew to remember and note it for he was a former tax collector. Scripture scholar, John L. McKenzie writes: "Rome at this period did not tax Roman citizens; the revenues of the government were obtained by taxing allies, provinces, and satellite kingdoms." Jesus is therefore making the analogy that, because he is the Son of God and therefore the heir apparent to his Father's house, he and his disciples are privileged people in the temple, as the Roman citizens are in the country. Jesus and his group, therefore, are not strictly obligated to pay the temple tax. The annual temple tax for an adult Jew was a half-shekel. The "stater" found in the fish's mouth was equal to a shekel. It paid the annual tax for two. Like Jesus, we often may not be absolutely bound to do a particular deed, but we do. Our motive is not obligation but edification.

TUESDAY, NINETEENTH WEEK OF THE YEAR
Ezk 2:8 - 3:4 and Mt 18:1-5, 10, 12-14

Many religious authors write and lecture on how to develop in the spiritual life and become holy. We might call such growth Christian maturity, spiritual development or simply living like Jesus. This Gospel says that the path to holiness and to becoming pleasing in God's sight is not complicated. We don't need to worry about trying to imitate some saintly person or to live a style of life that is foreign to us. Jesus says, remember what you were when you were a child and be like that again. The entrance into the kingdom is contingent upon our ability to "change and become like little children." Jesus, as an adult, is constantly in touch with his Father and sees his mission as doing the Father's will. In so doing, the Lord is demonstrating both trust and obedience. When we were children we most likely had a trusting spontaneity, a non-conditional giving kind of love and an excitement about the future. We simply assumed our parents would do the right things out of love and care for us. Now, as adults, we direct those same feelings of trust to God. Finding spiritual fulfillment does not so much mean capturing the future as it does recapturing the past.

WEDNESDAY, NINETEENTH WEEK OF THE YEAR
Ezk 9:1-7; 10, 18-22 and Mt 18:15-20

Today's Gospel presents a Christian formula which can be used to solve problems, mend divisions, and promote unity. First of all, we must have some kind of a dispute or disagreement with another. We don't have to search long to find that. When we're in the middle of a dispute we often complain to others, trying to garner sympathy for our side. In doing this we are stoking the fires of anger which inflames feelings of hatred and leads to thoughts of revenge. Jesus recommends this three-point remedy: (1) Schedule a "one to one" talk with the person involved. This certainly is a step in the right direction and often the only step needed. (2) If difficulties continue call a mutual friend, counselor, or anyone whose judgment you both respect and the three of you have a discussion. (3) Perhaps the problem still continues. Then call upon a group of people from the Church for assistance. Let the impartial group make some observations and judgments. When we have completed these three steps, if the difficulty continues, Jesus says we have done all that is expected. We just won't be friends, but it's not because we didn't try. Circumstances may cause us to vary the formula, but these three points give us a spiritual format to follow.

THURSDAY, NINETEENTH WEEK OF THE YEAR
Ezk 12:1-2 and Mt 18:21-19:1

On Feb. 11, 1935, an American school teacher by the name of Mira Moon was struck by a Japanese taxicab. The accident occurred in Tokyo where she taught English in a small college. She knew the seriousness of her injuries and quickly made a will. Mira died two days later and this was in her will: "Please do not punish the young taxi driver, because he has a future. Please give him all the money in my savings account because I understand that he is sending his salary to his elderly parents, living in the country. If he loses his job because of this accident, please ask some of my friends running trading companies in Tokyo to hire him as a chauffeur." A young Japanese businessman, who knew Miss Moon, has tried to discover more about her during these many years. He knows she was a native of Cleveland, Ohio. If he can't find a relative, he wants to send his information to a church in Cleveland to keep alive this story of Mira Moon's legacy of forgiving love. Peter asked if he should forgive his brother seven times. "No," Jesus replied, "not seven times; I say, seventy times seven times."

FRIDAY, NINETEENTH WEEK OF THE YEAR
Ezk 16:1-15, 60, 63 and Mt 19:3-12

Jesus says the establishment of divorce is a concession on the part of God. It was not intended from the beginning. The Lord strongly opposed divorce. To emphasize the unique and binding nature of marriage, we now refer to it as a covenant rather than use the older term of contract. A covenant means an agreement. A matrimonial covenant is an unretractable promise to be faithful and loving to each other until death. The visual reminder of the covenant is the wedding ring; a continuous circle, symbolizing undying devotion. The ring is worn on the third finger of the left hand, following an ancient belief that this finger is directly connected to the heart by the *"vena amoris,"* the vein of love. Jesus makes this teaching very clear to his disciples. Everything about marriage revolves around the circle of love and friendship, from the two in one, to the one family, the common property and united purpose. As the wedding ring, so the earthly duration of the covenant is never ending. The enduring unity of marriage finds a model in God's own covenant with us. Jesus made a lasting promise: "I will be with you always until the end of time."

SATURDAY, NINETEENTH WEEK OF THE YEAR
Ezk 18:1-10, 13, 30-32 and Mt 19:13-15

It's so easy to blame others for our woes. One political administration reprimands the preceding one for current difficulties. The present generation often finds fault with the manner in which things were done in the past. Ezekiel says people did the same thing in his time, which was in the sixth century B.C. They had a proverb in those days which is quoted in this passage. "Fathers have eaten green grapes, thus their children's teeth are on edge." It means the children are paying for the indiscretions of their parents. We have a modern day phrase which counterbalances this attitude of blaming others. We are told "to take ownership of" a particular idea or project. That means we should support endeavors with all the conviction and enthusiasm possible; as if the whole project had been conceived, born and brought to maturity by our own personal efforts. We would do well to see our contemporary world with all its ramifications handed down to us personally from God. Individual accountability to society has been tremendously weakened. If we would stop blaming others and take ownership of our personal responsibilities, the world would take an unbelievable turn for the better.

MONDAY, TWENTIETH WEEK OF THE YEAR
Ezk 24:15-24 and Mt 19:16-22

Here is a man who wants to explore the spiritual life deeply and to live it in all its fullness. Many living as piously as this individual, would feel satisfied that they were already experiencing a rich spiritual life. But not this person. He was a very wealthy person from a material point of view and he wanted to be just as affluent spiritually. We know people often give up the hope of being spiritually rich for the sake of gaining material things. They cut corners, lie, steal and try to sexually "sleep their way" into a high position. This man was blessed for he had resorted to none of these and still became very well-to-do. Perhaps he had inherited his money. Nonetheless, he is to be congratulated for being both very rich and very moral. We can note his obvious sincerity from the fact that he approached the Lord in the first place. Then, when Jesus said to keep the commandments, he asked "Which ones?" Here Jesus gives a new twist to this man's thinking. He wants the best of both worlds but Jesus tells him that, in order to obtain the best of the spiritual, one must forsake the material world. It's a kind of toss-up between material or spiritual treasures. How much is eternal life worth? A million, a billion, five billion? Jesus says it's worth everything we have, our possessions, our efforts and time. It is even worth the life of Jesus.

TUESDAY, TWENTIETH WEEK OF THE YEAR
Ezk 28:1-10 and Mt 19:23-30

In Latin, the word, *centum,* means one hundred. It is used often in the English language with the ending "um" dropped. A good example is the word percent (*per centum*). So whenever we speak of a percent, it means a part of a hundred. Every percentage starts from the base of one hundred. Peter, therefore, reminds Jesus that the apostles have given up a hundred percent: all their family, friends and common possessions for the sake of following him. The Lord, in turn, promises that the one hundred percent will be returned, plus many times more. In effect, he is saying that the more we "invest," i.e., give up, the more we will receive in return. Jesus promises we will receive back what we give up, plus the gift of eternal life. In this light the concluding remark is like saying that the current "have nots" will have an abundance; while those who now have, will eventually have not. This passage, similar to yesterday's, teaches us that there is a very real difficulty between being very rich and very spiritual. Material possessions do give a sense, albeit at times a false sense, of security. Jesus calls us to forsake that security and live by faith. This will bring real security to our lives now and lasting blessings hereafter.

WEDNESDAY, TWENTIETH WEEK OF THE YEAR
Ezk 34:1-11 and Mt 20:1-16

The shepherd theme is one of the Lord's favorites in the New Testament. Here in Ezekiel we discover the origin of some of the ideas which Jesus would later develop. The imagery is strikingly vivid. In this passage God upbraids the shepherds for pasturing themselves, instead of the sheep. Although usually praised by Jesus, the shepherds were often less than virtuous in their conduct. They would sometimes allow the sheep to eat another's grass, thus saving their own. That would be a clear example of shepherds "pasturing" themselves. Shepherds did not have the best reputation with the common people. When Jesus called himself the "Good Shepherd," he was contrasting himself with the disgraceful ones who would allow their sheep to feed in pasture ground which was not their own in order to enrich themselves at others' expense. Here, the prophet Ezekiel is looking into the future and seeing the distant coming of the Messiah. Jesus, we know, did actually become the universal shepherd for all people. He has led his flock, protected them in danger and died in their behalf. Jesus came, not to pasture or enrich himself at anyone else's expense, but to give himself as a ransom for the many. Today, we can individually acknowledge that the Lord is truly our shepherd.

THURSDAY, TWENTIETH WEEK OF THE YEAR
Ezk 36:23-28 and Mt 22:1-14

Ezekiel, here, is the messenger of hope for those who have been deported to Babylon to live in exile. Even though the exiled people did not suffer from severe physical torture, they always had mental suffering. Their whole value system had been destroyed and they would not be free until it was restored. They believed in One God and here they were being subjected to many gods. They believed in one united people and now they were divided and torn asunder. They felt they could not be at peace until they were at home, living on their own ground. Even if the exile would have subjected them to the severest of physical punishments, the mental and spiritual pains would have been worse. The prophet Ezekiel, therefore, was ministering to them in their most needed area. He was preaching a message of hope for better days ahead. Christianity is also future orientated. We are always hopeful of acquiring a new and better spirit; a kinder and more tender heart. The Church today, as Ezekiel in the past, calls us ever to be more dedicated to God as his holy people.

FRIDAY, TWENTIETH WEEK OF THE YEAR
Ezk 37:1-14 and Mt 22:34-40

"The foot bone connects to the leg bone, the leg bone connects to the knee bone, the knee bone connects to the thigh bone, the thigh bone connects to the hip bone, now hear the word of the Lord." We've all heard this moving spiritual. The song rhythmically relates how these dry and lifeless bones are reconnected with sinews and covered with flesh. Eventually, life returns to these dead people in the valley, resulting in a magnificent resurrection. That famous song owes its inspiration to this section of Ezekiel, which has helped to make it one of the most well-known passages in his book. Ezekiel here is preaching to the exiled citizens of his country who are both helpless and hopeless. What is more bereft of life than a pile of dry, sun-bleached bones? Yet out of just such a situation, by the power of God, hope blossoms into a new life-filled existence. This prophesy speaks more of a national renewal than a personal resurrection. Ezekiel, today, can be an inspiration to our country. In spite of all our ills, drugs, crimes, and troubles, society can find renewed hope and life through mutual human cooperation and God's blessings. ". . . now hear the word of the Lord."

SATURDAY, TWENTIETH WEEK OF THE YEAR
Ezk 43:1-7 and Mt 23:1-12

Jesus, a person who was both meek and humble of heart, was not always that way with everyone. To the hurting and helpless, yes; but he reserved some of his most severe condemnations for the scribes and Pharisees. There existed a certain natural animosity between them. In the light of that observation, I find the opening sentence of this passage to be absolutely remarkable. It shows the tremendous fairness and objectivity of Jesus. The Lord tells both the crowds and even his own disciples to observe everything the scribes and Pharisees teach. His reasoning, because they have a legitimate teaching office and have succeeded Moses in that capacity, they are teaching that which is true. Quickly, however, he adds, "But do not follow their example." It is natural to be totally opposed to someone with whom we are in bitter, public opposition. Imagine two people engaged in a heated debate and one of the participants paying a genuine compliment to the opponent. Jesus calmly and objectively approves their good qualities and defends their position while, at the same time, he exposes their glaring faults. How many of us could make that delicate distinction in dealing with people? We, like Jesus, must be guided not by personal feelings but by the unbiased truth.

MONDAY, TWENTY-FIRST WEEK OF THE YEAR
2 Th 1:1-5, 11-12 and Mt 23:13-22

This passage in Matthew begins a series of seven woes. The word "woe," as used here by Jesus, means a prediction of misfortune on someone. He wants the scribes and Pharisees to be more spirit-filled and less legalistic. A threat of punishment is promised if they continue to lay heavy spiritual burdens upon the people. Their cold and heartless teachings infuriate his normally mild temperament. Jesus calls them "frauds, . . . twice as wicked as the devil, . . . blind guides . . . and blind fools." One needs not read very far to catch his vindictive tone. This condemnation points out some of the minute and legalistic practices which constituted pharisaism at its worst. It shows the endless and futile distinctions which they bickered over from their narrow legalistic point of view. Jesus wants people to live by the spirit of the law rather than to be scrupulous about the exact letter. Basic to this discussion is the fact that we do not earn our salvation, as pharisaical legalism would teach. Salvation is a pure gift, flowing from the spilled blood of Jesus. We avoid being religious frauds by trusting in the loving kindness of our Savior and living our life in that faith.

TUESDAY, TWENTY-FIRST WEEK OF THE YEAR
2 Th 2:1-3, 14-16 and Mt 23:23-26

Jesus has set aside his kid gloves in this passage. He wades into the Pharisees and swings at them with both fists. He hits them with the dual accusations of frauds and blind guides. A blind person needs to be guided. So he's really saying that the Pharisees who are the guides are really imposters for they, themselves, need someone to lead them. A blind person can not lead another along the road in safety. The Pharisees, therefore, are hazardous to the safety of the people. They simply don't qualify as guides and mentors. Jesus, by contrast, comes with the credentials of being the all-seeing God and the enlightened guide. Jesus liberates people, while the Pharisees enslave them. All things must be judged and done in proper perspective. We might think that how we dress for church is more important than the dispositions of our hearts. Our private devotions may be preferred to the practices of faith, hope, love and service. This would be an example of "straining out the gnat and swallowing the camel." Perspective is the key concept for a balanced spirituality and life in general.

WEDNESDAY, TWENTY-FIRST WEEK OF THE YEAR
2 Th 3:6-10, 16-18 and Mt 23:27-32

A rather well-known movie actor was being interviewed on television. When asked how he felt physically, he replied that his health was failing. "But you look so good," the host said. "Well, that's the most important thing," the actor answered. "It's not how well you feel but how well you look." With a smile the host interjected, "I think you mean that the other way around don't you? It's not how well you look but how you feel." The actor immediately replied, "No, I meant it the way I said it. I just always want to look good and make a fine appearance, regardless of how lousy I really feel." That dialogue came to mind when reading today's Gospel. The Pharisees must have thought in the same vein as the actor. Their main concern was to give the appearance of a holy exterior, even though within they were filled with "hypocrisy and evil." Jesus looks through the exterior to see the true image of what we are. It's natural to want to impress others with a good image. It's very spiritual to concentrate on the interior life and see that as the true reality.

THURSDAY, TWENTY-FIRST WEEK OF THE YEAR
1 Cor 1:1-9 and Mt 24:42-51

Today, we begin reading Paul's first letter to the Corinthians. It will continue as our epistle readings for the next twenty days. Paul had preached in this most important Greek city and stayed there about eighteen months — longer than he did in any other city. Later he wrote to them at least two letters — a third one has been lost. The scholars believe Paul was there in the year 51 A.D. and wrote the first letter about 56 A.D. There is no other New Testament book which reveals so much about its author as well as the community. Corinth had a multifaceted reputation. Homer had spoken of it as "wealthy Corinth" and Cicero called Corinth "the light of all Greece." It, likewise, was known for its licentiousness. If it were said that someone was living like a Corinthian, it meant that he or she was living a dissolute life and the term "Corinthian girl" was a euphemism for a prostitute. Here Paul was challenged to test the power of God's love. In spite of all the negative odds against success, Paul achieved remarkable results. We have the same faith as Paul; it can enable us also to overcome what may seem insurmountable odds.

FRIDAY, TWENTY-FIRST WEEK OF THE YEAR
1 Cor 1:17-25 and Mt 25:1-13

The ancient Palestinian wedding ceremonies were much different from ours. (1) The groom first went to the home of his future bride at night and talked to her father. (2) Then the bride and groom together came to their own home to celebrate. (3) The bridesmaids would go out with their torches to wait for and welcome them, then escort them into their own home. (4) Following that, the door was closed and barred for the night. It was no small task to open the heavy door, once it had been barred shut. The moral of the parable of the ten virgins is that we are to be prepared and think ahead. The application is made to entrance into the kingdom of Heaven. Jesus is often seen as the groom and the people in the Church represent the bride. We are warned to avoid the conduct of the foolish bridesmaids and imitate the wise. Liturgically, we now prepare to welcome and be welcomed by the groom. We want to be locked into the kingdom, not locked outside in the darkness.

SATURDAY, TWENTY-FIRST WEEK OF THE YEAR
1 Cor 1:26-31 and Mt 25:14-30

Previously, we noted that the city of Corinth was very cosmopolitan. Natives and visitors of every type, class, color and social degree abounded in its streets and participated in the variety of activities which were available. From the tone of Paul's letter, we would conclude that the group which joined the Christian church was rather mediocre. He says not many of them were wise, influential or wellborn. These, however, are the ones whom God has chosen, not only for the benefit of their own salvation but especially to teach the "high society — upper class people" what it truly means to be "high class." The Greeks had their gods and goddesses but their philosophy taught that there was no way these divine beings intervened in human affairs on earth. Paul, therefore, makes the point that he is teaching an entirely new message and asking them to reconsider one of the basic principles upon which they based their lives. God, in Jesus, has intervened in human life for the uplifting of the human condition. If the lowly can be lifted up from their status as nobodies to that of those who possess wisdom, justice, holiness and salvation, then this is good news for everyone.

MONDAY, TWENTY-SECOND WEEK OF THE YEAR
1 Cor 2:1-5 and Lk 4:16-30

This passage reveals some clear insights into the nature of Jesus. (1) He had the habit of worshipping every week in the synagogue on the Sabbath. (2) He participated in the worship by doing the reading. Those of you who read the Scriptures at the liturgy of the word perform a dignified service. Jesus, too, was a lector. (3) He knew the Scriptures and applied them to various circumstances. In other words he planned the liturgy. (4) Jesus saw himself as the Messiah and knew that this Scripture passage actually referred to him. (5) We see his guiding light and sense of mission. (6) Not accepted by his hometown people, Jesus is not alarmed or revengeful. He understands human nature. (7) The Lord copes with violence by making a peaceful response. This Scripture passage offers a penetrating insight into the nature of Jesus. It could serve as an excellent text for meditation, personal development or group discussion.

TUESDAY, TWENTY-SECOND WEEK OF THE YEAR
1 Cor 2:10-16 and Lk 4:31-37

This Gospel passage immediately follows yesterday's and is contrasted to it. Yesterday, we had the account of Jesus being hatefully ejected from the synagogue in Nazareth. Now he is in Capernaum, which is not far from Nazareth and the people love him and are spellbound by his speech. Jesus is praised, for he speaks with authority and confidence and that gives the people courage. Here, in Capernaum, Jesus can work miracles and drive out evil spirits. Even the evil spirits call him "the holy one of God." The more Jesus did, the more the people believed, which in turn enabled Jesus to do even more. None of this was done in Nazareth because they did not believe in Jesus. Two synagogues with two totally different personalities. They are only a few miles apart in terms of physical distance but a world apart in their approach to Jesus. Our churches can be similar. Each have their own theological personalities which reflect the ways they have been formed over the years. How important it is for people to be formed not according to the biases of a few but to receive the correct Gospel outlook. Pastors have a grave responsibility to lead congregations in the true spirit of Jesus.

WEDNESDAY, TWENTY-SECOND WEEK OF THE YEAR
1 Cor 3:1-9 and Lk 4:38-44

We don't teach algebra and calculus to children in the first grade. These and other more challenging subjects will come later. Paul uses that same type of analogy to explain his choice of the spiritual teachings he imparted to the Corinthians. Milk, not solid food, he says is what they need at present. They were still spiritual infants, still struggling to overcome their petty jealousies and foolish quarrels. As we mature in age, we should also make a conscious effort to acquire equal progress in spiritual areas. As children we might have been fascinated with little devotional practices and pious stories. Perhaps those formed the outer limits of our concept of religion. As adults we must move beyond that into the more mature areas of the deeper mysteries of life, assessing the future, exploring the nature of God and learning how to live saintly lives of justice, service and peace. Some Christians don't want to chew solid food, but are content to sip only milk all their lives. We need to keep growing spiritually so that we, as adults, can make better informed judgments and religious choices than we did as children.

THURSDAY, TWENTY-SECOND WEEK OF THE YEAR
1 Cor 3:18-23 and Lk 5:1-11

This Gospel contrasts the difference between acting from professional knowledge and following the dictates of faith. Human intelligence and logic certainly are to be taken into consideration in making our life's decisions. That being said, the intelligent and logical course to pursue is sometimes simply to follow the path of faith. The world of faith calls us to make decisions concerning matters which we do not yet clearly see. The situation is beyond our grasp, out of our sight, below the water. Jesus was definitely an authority on matters of religion but the apostles were the professionals when it came to fishing. According to everything they had ever learned, this was not the right time to fish. Nor was it the correct place, for there they had labored fruitlessly all night long. Though professional fishermen, they were still novices in the ways of faith and so it was with reluctance that they obeyed the Lord's challenge to put out into the deep once more and throw in their nets. But in doing so, they all took a major step forward in their growth as men of faith. Gradually, they would learn to trust and obey the voice of the One who could see beneath the surface even though that advice seemed to be contrary to human wisdom.

FRIDAY, TWENTY-SECOND WEEK OF THE YEAR
1 Cor 4:1-5 and Lk 5:33-39

One of the things we often do and do wrongly is to pass judgment on other people. It just seems to be a part of our nature. Scripture, in many places and in many ways, says it's a dangerous activity. In this passage, Paul warns the Corinthians about judging others. He says, "I do not even pass judgment on myself." If we could simply allow others to be responsible to themselves and presume they are sincere and doing their best, we could free ourselves of a tremendous weight we often carry within. Is it really so important that we worry what others are saying about us? People are free to mention our names and make comments, if they like, and we don't have a right to inquire what is being said, or to make them stop. In regard to discussing others and being discussed ourselves, we could find a whole lot of inner peace if we would simply be true to ourselves. As Paul tells us, God is the one and only judge we have and God judges only after looking into the heart. If all is well there, who needs to worry about what others think or say?

SATURDAY, TWENTY-SECOND WEEK OF THE YEAR
1 Cor 4:9-15 and Lk 6:1-5

Paul was not opposed to bragging about his life and work. By so doing, he sometimes gave a certain "witness preaching" which moved others also to draw closer to Jesus. Here, Paul is bragging about his own life and that of other apostles in a negative manner. He says there's a wide contrast between how the apostles are attempting to live as opposed to the average Christian of the city of Corinth. The people have divided themselves into factions, each group judging itself better than the others. The apostle tells them to stop thinking about how high class they are and to begin thinking more in terms of what followers of Jesus should be. The apostles are the best examples of those who are truly trying to be like Jesus. They consider themselves fools for the sake of Christ. They are also weak, hungry, thirsty and poorly clothed. Church leaders are expected to have a humble view of their lives and be willing to suffer as Jesus did. All Christians would do well to think in these same terms. We would all take a major step forward if we cease considering our degree of importance and realize that Jesus is the only one really important Christian.

MONDAY, TWENTY-THIRD WEEK OF THE YEAR
1 Cor 5:1-8 and Lk 6:6-11

Lewd conduct was commonplace in Corinth. The problem is, it's now happening within the Christian community. Paul had clearly explained to the new converts their moral responsibilities before they were baptized. Now he is angry to hear about this incestuous union in a Christian family, between a young man and his stepmother. The Apostle stresses the serious sinfulness involved, stating that this type of conduct isn't tolerated even among the pagans. It was understood that situations of this nature should be referred to the Church for a hearing and solution. Paul was a strong believer that the Christian community could and should solve their own problems, without soliciting outside assistance. The community in this case had taken no corrective action, thereby showing a certain tolerance which further irritated Paul. He, therefore, makes the decision that the offender is to be punished in order that he may be saved. We can only speculate what Paul's reaction would be to all that's happening in our society today. The modern day Christian is often expected to reject that which the world approves. The spirit of Paul still offers us enlightenment and courage.

TUESDAY, TWENTY-THIRD WEEK OF THE YEAR
1 Cor 6:1-11 and Lk 6:12-19

Paul wanted the community itself to settle a moral problem in yesterday's Scripture reading. Now he is asking the Christians of Corinth to resolve a lawsuit, not in the civil courts, but in the Church. Again he shows his deep faith in the collective wisdom of the Church members. We would do well to reflect on the faith we possess in our various congregations. Do we have the tremendous faith of Paul? Paul, here, teaches that Christians are to be sharers in Christ's royal power and participate in the judgment of the world. That same objective had been requested earlier by the mother of James and John. She had wanted Jesus to situate her two sons on each side of him in a position of power and judgment. The same idea occurs in Revelation, where the saints are pictured on thrones judging the world. Flowing out of this thinking, Paul reasons, if Christians are capable of these universal judgments, they certainly should be able to arrive at the right decision in a much lesser matter. The derivation of the word judge is literally, "to decide what is right." The Lord asks us collectively to be judges in our own affairs.

WEDNESDAY, TWENTY-THIRD WEEK OF THE YEAR
1 Cor 7:25-31 and Lk 6:20-26

The Beatitudes which we generally read in the liturgy are from Matthew's fifth chapter. Matthew pictures Jesus sitting down — as teachers used to do in Palestine — with his apostles and disciples gathered around. He spoke to them about the people who were lowly, poor, etc. They might have discussed the situation and inquired about some ways they could help them. Luke's account of the beatitudes makes them much more personal to the group at hand. He sees Jesus saying, blessed are *you* who are poor, *you* who hunger, etc. Now, it's very personalized. We should read it as something personal, also. Imagine Jesus speaking to you, personally, and the passage takes on a richer meaning. Note that the woes are also personalized. The last one especially is revealing: "Woe when all speak well of you." If that's the case, compliments perhaps should make us very nervous. We might think that it's a good sign of our virtue when others speak well of us, but it could also indicate that we are acting like hypocrites, as were the false prophets. Blessed are those who speak not to please people, but to convey truth.

THURSDAY, TWENTY-THIRD WEEK OF THE YEAR
1 Cor 8:1-7, 11-13 and Lk 6:27-38

This scriptural passage refers to God by the name of "The Most High." There are certain obligations placed upon us, which must be fulfilled in order to be called children of "The Most High." These requirements are: to love our enemies; do good; and lend without expecting repayment. These may seem easy, but in reality they are very hard. To achieve them we will be pushed to a heroic degree for they are extremely difficult and go against all our natural inclinations. There is no natural motive for loving our enemies; only a supernatural one. The supernatural motive is to imitate God, for "The Most High" is "good to the ungrateful and the wicked." It's tough enough being kind to the ungrateful — those who never show appreciation or express their thankfulness. It's even more difficult being kind to the wicked. They are not only ungrateful but actually give trouble to the one who is being kind to them. Those are the enemies. Children of "The Most High" turn the other cheek and walk the extra mile. They also give the shirts off their backs and do not expect them to be returned. Do we live like the children of "The Most High"?

FRIDAY, TWENTY-THIRD WEEK OF THE YEAR
1 Cor 9:16-19; 22-27 and Lk 6:39-42

There's a compulsion within most of us to produce, excel or achieve something. When we start a project, we want to see it completed and really push ourselves toward that objective. Perhaps, I have ten articles or talks to write within the next week. I get one completed and immediately I want to complete another and then another. We may be remodelling our home. It's time to quit and get our sleep but we often want to finish this wall, hang that light or get the sink in place. We have a compulsion to get the job done. The same is true with reading a book. We know we've read enough for the day but "just one more page," we say, and then another. Paul explains it's like that with his preaching. "I am under compulsion and have no choice." In his comparison to a runner, Paul says his mind also is only on the finish line. Paul's finish line or goal is to make as many people aware of Jesus as he possibly can. When our goals are greatly desirable and our minds are firmly set on achieving them, then all hardships are diminished. For what goals and objectives are we willing to suffer in order to achieve them?

SATURDAY, TWENTY-THIRD WEEK OF THE YEAR
1 Cor 10:14-22 and Lk 6:43-49

Very recently, a couple in their late twenties were planning their wedding ceremony. They had selected readings from Fr. Champlain's fine book, *Together for Life.* From the 10 different Gospel passages listed, they chose the story which we read today about the house built upon a rock. Although the passage doesn't mention anything about husbands and wives, love or marriage, they definitely wanted that Gospel. The groom said, "We're trying to lay the best foundation for our future which we possibly can." He then added, "If we can base our marriage on a solid foundation, everything else will work out OK." One has to be impressed by their thoughtfulness. Jesus laid a good foundation for his Church and so Christianity has outlived all who tried to destroy it. A solid foundation is necessary in every building, especially the building of our spiritual lives. The various kinds of floods, torrents and winds are forceful and numerous, but stronger yet, is the divine promise. A firm foundation of faith in God and love of others will enable us to withstand and prosper, despite negative elements.

MONDAY, TWENTY-FOURTH WEEK OF THE YEAR
1 Cor 11:17-26, 33 and Lk 7:1-10

The term "worth" has a basic meaning which is "to become." If I would say, "I'm not worth much as a singer or artist," there is a hint in that statement that I want to become better. When we refer to an individual as being "a worthy," it means that such an individual is a prominent person. In this Gospel, when the centurion says he's not worthy for Jesus to come into his house, he's saying that he is not a Jewish person and he doesn't want Jesus to compromise his standards by entering the house of a Gentile. It's also implied here, if ever so slightly, that the centurion may want to become a follower of Jesus. At present he is "a worthy" in the eyes of many people, especially his soldiers, but he's still trying to become worthy in the presence of Jesus. Our old hymn, "O Lord, I am not worthy," again is not a total put-down of one's self but a prayerful expression of our hope that through God's grace and our efforts we may someday be much more worthy. We express at every Mass, prior to Holy Communion that we are not worthy to have the Lord come to us. At the same time, we recall what God's eternal word has also said, namely, that we have been purified and made whole by his saving grace.

TUESDAY, TWENTY-FOURTH WEEK OF THE YEAR
1 Cor 12:12-14, 27-31 and Lk 7:11-17

We emphasize the qualities of our churches in many ways. Some speak of their large attendance, others of their many organizations, or efficient staff. One elderly lady highlighted what she liked best about her church in this way: "You know, when a person joins this church, from that moment on, you never have to bear another burden alone." Paul gives the Corinthians that same message when he says the Church has one uniting Spirit that binds the people together. They are all members of one unified body of Christ. There, they find strength, not only from God, but from each other. In a sense, if one is a part of the group, that person never needs to bear his or her burdens alone, for the group will give support. There is present, in this one body, a multi-talented group of gifted individuals. That's what a congregation is — a gathering together of many kinds of people. The key force which holds all the members together in the body of Christ is the Spirit. We have many differences from each other, but share the same Spirit. It is the Spirit that unites us to bear each other's burdens.

WEDNESDAY, TWENTY-FOURTH WEEK OF THE YEAR
1 Cor 12:31 - 13:13 and Lk 7:31-35

This Corinthian text has to be one of the most famous and often quoted passages in the entire Bible. It speaks of the real meaning of love and, therefore, is a natural choice to be read at numerous weddings. But we should note well, this famous text was not composed for those planning to be married. It was written to be the guiding light for all Christians. Originally it was meant for those living in the wide open city of Corinth and, from there, it spread its guiding influence to the entire world. Love has many different meanings but here it's described so simply: "Love is patient; love is kind." What follows from there is a kind of commentary on the words patient and kind. All these marvelous qualities of love gives it, as is stated in the last sentence of the paragraph, the "power to endure." It often takes us a long time to personally come to terms with the pure wisdom of this passage. I might be very much afraid to trust my future success to patience and kindness. In some ways, I'm more secure with using harshness and maybe some violence, if necessary. However love continues to be victorious and, finally, I see that's the best approach.

THURSDAY, TWENTY-FOURTH WEEK OF THE YEAR
1 Cor 15:1-11 and Lk 7:36-50

Paul uses an insightful time-sequence in this passage to the Corinthians. He refers to having preached the Gospel to them at sometime in the past. Now, a considerable while later, they are "being saved by it at this very time . . ." So often these days we hear people witnessing how they were saved at a particular place and time. It is referred to as an instantaneous happening. Paul seems to say here that a person is continually being saved, if such a one keeps living the message which was preached. Being saved, therefore, is not a one time happening, but an ongoing conversion. Salvation comes as grace and power swirl about us each day, continuing to deepen our love of God and practice of virtue. The sacred message preached by Paul, which brought salvation to the Corinthians, is the same one which is bringing salvation to us at this very moment. It's the age-old message that Christ died for our sins and rose from the dead. According to that interpretation, we should be "more saved" this evening than we were this morning.

FRIDAY, TWENTY-FOURTH WEEK OF THE YEAR
1 Cor 15:12-20 and Lk 8:1-3

Several years ago, the Princeton Research Center studied peoples' attitudes concerning life after death. The findings showed that 70% of Americans believe in some form of eternal life. We may think that would be about the average around the world. Surprisingly, in Denmark and France, only about 25% of the people believe in an afterlife. Paul says if Christ had not been raised from the dead, then all of our preaching would have been in vain and our faith would be useless. It seems an exaggeration to say our faith would be useless if Christ had not arisen. Many times Jesus spoke in a figurative or poetic manner and if he would not have risen from the dead I would think the Church might have thought he was speaking about physical resurrection also in a figurative way. Suppose Jesus would not have physically risen, still his spirit would have been alive, so perhaps his teaching would still have endured. Many religions flourish today, whose founders or foundresses never bodily rose from the grave. The resurrection places the total seal of approval on everything Jesus did and said and helps us to find many reasons to be solid in our faith.

SATURDAY, TWENTY-FOURTH WEEK OF THE YEAR
1 Cor 1:15, 35-37, 42-49 and Lk 8:4-15

This Pauline passage makes a point by reflecting back to the time of Adam and Eve, a story well-known to all. It concerns the origin of the human race, and recalls that period, which was very short-lived, when Adam and Eve dwelt on a high and happy plane. They were defeated by the tempter and lost paradise. Here, the first Adam of Genesis is contrasted with Jesus, the second (or last) Adam. The first stood for everything natural, weak and temporary. The last Adam was just opposite. He was beyond the natural, so he could therefore uplift the fallen natural man. The last Adam was strong and didn't fall to the tempter which drove the first Adam out of Paradise. The first Adam was a living soul, while the last Adam was a life-giving spirit. Everything which is supernatural and spiritual is based on the natural. The spiritual is the perfection of the natural. The last Adam fulfills all that was lacking in the first and leads the human race to the perfection and fulfillment, which, otherwise, would never have been possible. It is sad that the first Adam fell in defeat, but had he not, the last Adam would not have come. We might, therefore, have never known what limitless possibilities for perfection exist within humankind. O Happy Fault!

MONDAY, TWENTY-FIFTH WEEK OF THE YEAR
Pr 3:27-34 and Lk 8:16-18

Several years ago when on vacation in Springfield, Illinois, we walked past the restored home of Abraham Lincoln at night. The lights were on in the house and you could almost imagine seeing the tall figure of the President inside, walking from his desk to the rocking chair. The entire atmosphere took one back to the middle of the nineteenth century, when Lincoln and his family lived there. The lights in the house and street seemed to speak a meaningful message, all their own. I read about a mother and her little child passing this same national shrine at night when it was brightly lighted. "Look mama," the child uttered excitedly, "Mr. Lincoln left his lights on." The mother answered, "Yes, he left them on for the whole world to see." Lincoln's lights are still glowing, but the brightest light is the person himself. His common sense and deeds of goodness are truly legendary. In today's Gospel, Jesus encourages all people to be lights of the world. We are not to hide our lights but make them bright and lift them high. It is the nature of a light to shine and help the world to find its way through the darkness.

TUESDAY, TWENTY-FIFTH WEEK OF THE YEAR
Pr 21:1-6, 10-13 and Lk 8:19-21

This passage from Proverbs is filled with practical instructions which are expressed in beautiful poetry. The person, who thinks he or she is always correct, must think twice, for here we are told it doesn't matter what we think, it's God who judges the heart. Consider the person who constantly lies in his business dealings in order to make more money. Before he knows, his devious ways will bring about his downfall. The proverb says: ". . . trying to make a fortune by a lying tongue is like chasing a bubble over deadly snares." Our devious plans will fall and break. The Hebrew mind thought only in concrete, poetic images rather than in abstract ideas. Such a way of thinking produces pictures which remain in the mind long after the sounds have departed the ears. Picture the scene in the last verse. Someone places his hands over his ears so he won't hear the poor crying out in pain and hunger. Later, this man will be in want and cry out and others will cover their ears and leave him unministered to in his state of agony. It's a clear, vivid picture of the golden rule.

WEDNESDAY, TWENTY-FIFTH WEEK OF THE YEAR
Pr 30:5-9 and Lk 9:1-6

The author of Proverbs in this passage tells God that he desires only the simplest things in life. He wants just enough food to live on, no more. If he has too much, he may be tempted to feel proud and deny his absolute dependency on God. Yet he wants enough food because if he doesn't have enough, he may be tempted to steal. Thereby, he would offend God. One thing we must say in favor of this person; he certainly does understand himself and has a true picture of his strengths and weaknesses. Many, dreaming of the good things of life, would like to win the lottery or some other vast sum of money. We tend to think of the winners as not only instantly rich but also instantly happy. That is pure fantasy and wishful thinking on their part and ours. Sometimes the more we have, the more miserable we become, for then we have more worries about what to do with our riches. Our sorrow increases when we think of dying and leaving it all behind. Those who have but little can be much more spiritual, for their treasure is the Lord and it is the Lord they hope to possess forever.

THURSDAY, TWENTY-FIFTH WEEK OF THE YEAR
Ec 1:2-11 and Lk 9:7-9

In this very famous passage, we hear the inner thoughts of Qoheleth. He has been called cynical, heretical, pessimistic and worldly. It is amazing that this book of Ecclesiastes is even found in the Bible at all, for its whole tone is very different from the other books. Qoheleth was most likely a teacher in the third century B.C. In this poetic passage, as in the entire book, he writes in a most realistic manner. His thoughts are directly centered on those things which he observes and experiences. He notes that there is an ever recurring sameness in life. To him, everything is monotonous, empty and dull. Our existence lacks any lasting meaning. Eventually, it will all end in a puff of smoke, and future generations will not remember those who lived before them. We can easily understand why he is labelled a pessimistic thinker and writer. At the same time, Qoheleth is a refreshing individual. He stands in direct contradiction to those who preach that all is rosy and lovely and that God cares for our every whim. We need to hear Qoheleth to give us a balanced view of reality. It's wonderful that such a book is found in the Bible.

FRIDAY, TWENTY-FIFTH WEEK OF THE YEAR
Ec 3:1-11 and Lk 9:18-22

For a number of years, Sam Shulsky wrote a newspaper column giving advice about investing and the use of money. In one column, he told an affluent widow that she had saved enough and should start spending. Later, another elderly reader objected. "Money should be saved," he said, "and one should practice self-denial." Shulsky replied that there is nothing wrong with self-denial when building a fund for retirement. "When one arrives at the age, it's time to be comfortable and if that includes spending some money on luxuries and little extras . . . I say go to it." He then quoted the few lines from Qoheleth which we read today. It is difficult for us to make transitions in our lives — to realize that there truly is "an appointed time for everything. A time to be born and a time to die. A time to plant and a time to uproot the plant." This well-known and often read poem of Sacred Scripture has become a popular song. It contains a penetrating assessment of reality which is good to recall during the various stages of our lives.

SATURDAY, TWENTY-FIFTH WEEK OF THE YEAR
Ec 11:9 - 12:8 and Lk 9:43-45

We now come to the end of Qoheleth's book. This is the final hymn to his observations on life. The Scripture commentator, James Fischer, C.M., calls this passage "one of the most hauntingly beautiful poems in all of literature." As he does throughout his book, Qoheleth, here again, pulls together the extremes in creation, enabling us to see them in one sweeping glance. Sunrise and sunset, darkness and light, the strength of youth and the weakness of old age, all find a place in his commentary on life. He talks of joy and sorrow, birth and death and feels obliged to encourage the young to enjoy their youth and to live it to the full. "Follow the ways of your heart, the vision of your eyes," he tells them. Before we know, the years will have gone, and what once seemed to be unending will soon be a fading memory. The last scene is hauntingly graphic. He speaks of that day when the "pitcher is shattered at the spring and the broken pulley falls into the well . . . the dust returns to the earth and the life breath returns to God who gave it." Contrary to Qoheleth's own teaching, though, all is not fleeting and forgotten. He is still remembered and read. His life was not empty and useless, for his insights continue to enrich us and make us think about our own lives and the purpose behind it all.

MONDAY, TWENTY-SIXTH WEEK OF THE YEAR
Jb 1:6-22 and Lk 9:46-50

This week our first readings at Mass and the homilies will pertain to the Book of Job. Numbered among the seven Wisdom Books of the Old Testament, the Book of Job presents various views about the problem of human suffering. Job is innocent of any wrongdoing and, yet, the most severe misfortunes fall upon him. His story is told in the framework of a dramatic poem which, today, ranks among the literary masterpieces of all times. In its forty-two brief chapters are found the feelings and struggles of all people who, like Job, question the adverse happenings in their lives and look for solutions. The anonymous author, writing about the 6th century B.C., presents Job as a pious oriental chieftain who suddenly loses domestic prosperity and personal dignity. The stated cause is a kind of contest between God and Satan. The two of them decide to test the true quality of Job's virtue and love of God. Satan says that Job will crumble in the face of suffering; God says he won't. In a series of five scenes, between heaven and earth, the stage is set. The ancients did not know why they had to suffer. We don't know either. The physical sufferings of the innocent remain one of our most elusive mysteries.

TUESDAY, TWENTY-SIXTH WEEK OF THE YEAR
Jb 3:1-3, 11-17, 20-23 and Lk 9:51-56R

After losing family and possessions, Job still does not turn against God. The test now bears directly upon his body as he is covered with painful boils. He still does not curse God. When his three friends fail to support him, Job finally loses his patience. That's where today's reading begins. He does not turn against God but curses the day he was born. He says it was a sad day when at his birth someone announced, "The child is a boy." He wishes he would have died at birth and not seen the light of day, for then he would have rest and peace. Job is now searching for death as one searches for a hidden treasure. We know that these same feelings are present in the hearts of many people today. They are found in those who are deeply depressed, who can see no way out except through death. To some extent we have all been down that path with Job. This reading can cause us to question ourselves about how best to cope with our sufferings, whatever nature they may be. It's very human to wish them away. Can we find meaningful spiritual helps to face our daily battles?

WEDNESDAY, TWENTY-SIXTH WEEK OF THE YEAR
Jb 9:1-12, 14-16 and Lk 9:57-62

Job's friends are narrow-minded and judgmental. They say he suffers because he has sinned. Their advice to him is to confess his sin and he will be healed. That was the current view at the time — personal suffering results from personal sin. Job denies his sinfulness. In this passage, Job replies to the speech of his friend, Bildad. Job sees himself in a helpless position before God. He wants to lash out in anger and blame God for his deteriorating condition but still he must admire the wisdom and power of God. This leaves him very frustrated. Lacking any satisfying answer from God, Job thinks perhaps he is under the influence of the constellations and stars and that they are causing his series of bad luck. Many in the ancient world looked to the stars for answers in their lives. In our lives there are those times, perhaps often, when we must endure these same feelings as Job. Tragedy comes in one form or another and we don't know the reason or the meaning. We, too, grope for answers. The best response is to keep faith in God's goodness and continue to trust.

THURSDAY, TWENTY-SIXTH WEEK OF THE YEAR
Jb 19:21-27 and Lk 10:1-12

Job looks for a vindicator, an avenger, who will bring punishment and retaliation to the one who has so severely injured him. In the tribal society of the Hebrew world, there was the office of Vindicator. The person who occupied this office had the responsibility of protecting the weaker members of the family. If they were offended, the vindicator would punish those who had caused the injury. In our society, it is the law which is expected to protect the weak and punish the guilty, but sometimes the law falls short. It was because of the law's ineptitude that the Mafia Godfather became so popular in the ghetto climate of the big cities where one ethnic group took up arms against another and one's own "family" needed protection. That, today, is a throwback to this old tribal position of Vindicator. Job had always trusted in God as his avenger, but now it seems like God is the one afflicting him. Centuries later, on the cross, Jesus would express those same sentiments and wonder if God had completely forsaken him. When we face our daily trials and think God has abandoned us, we need to have the patience of Job. Jesus, along with many others whom God loved intensely, were severely tested. Here, in today's passage, the patience of Job is nearly depleted and he wants to die, but somehow he still hangs on. So can we.

FRIDAY, TWENTY-SIXTH WEEK OF THE YEAR
Jb 38:1, 12-21, 40:3-5 and Lk 10:13-16

In the year 1710, G.W. Leibnitz wrote a book entitled *Theodicy*. He said the purpose of his work was to plead the cause of God. It was his expressed desire to show the goodness and omnipotence of God. He opposed those who said there can not be a good and kind God because of all the evils of earthly life. Leibnitz's title is from the Greek, which means "God's judgment." When we see physical evils and accidents happening today, we wonder about the goodness of God. It has always been a problem to explain, and the question continues to evade a suitable solution. Here, Job admits his powerlessness of both body and mind to solve his problem. In a gesture of surrender, he places his hand over his mouth saying he will not even speak of it anymore. He views the vast expansion of the universe and admits he is but a tiny creature. In comparison to the world about us, we are all tiny and insignificant. Job is silent and submissive, and still does not curse God. Like him, we, too, can be pushed to the very limits and still find hope to endure. Job does not tell us why we suffer but shows us how.

SATURDAY, TWENTY-SIXTH WEEK OF THE YEAR
Jb 42:1-3, 5-6, 12-16 and Lk 10:17-24

The book of Job now comes to an end. The liturgy has digested the forty-two chapters into six short readings for this past week. The precise question discussed has been: Why do innocent people suffer? The story has involved God, Satan, friends, questions, pain and, finally, total vindication. In the epistle of James (5:11), there is a reference to the steadfastness of Job and a reminder of what the compassion and merciful God did in the end. The book does answer one question: Is suffering the result of personal sin? The answer is a resounding, "No!" Job's friends, who reflect this frequently held position, are clearly seen to be wrong. The author of the Book of Job possesses penetrating insights into many key areas of life. In the format of this drama, those insightful views are given full rein. In spite of all our religious discussions, we still often feel that a personal misfortune is the result of some recent sin we have committed. Remember, the whole purpose of the book is to dispel that view. This 2600-year-old book can still give us courage for those unexplained pains of tomorrow.

MONDAY, TWENTY-SEVENTH WEEK OF THE YEAR
Gal 1:6-12 and Lk 10:25-37

   Self-preservation is an instinct. We didn't have to learn it. It is strong and enduring. It makes us eat, sleep and jump out of the way of speeding cars. The natural desire to save our lives makes us want to preserve them forever. The lawyer, therefore, inquires of Jesus how he can inherit everlasting life. The Old Testament law is restated. You are to give God the best you've got. Give your heart, which is the center of love. We are to love our way into eternity. Hate makes the entrance difficult. Give your soul, which is your life. That life was originally given by God and we are now simply to return it. Give your personal energies and good works. God is active in the world and we are to imitate God by being active, too. Give your mind — the intellectual center of your life. We are to use our highest powers for seeking the highest goals. Finally, in loving our neighbor as ourselves, we want only the best for others. Our love for neighbor is to be as strong as our own desire for self-preservation. It's a full-time job, Jesus says, to reach the kingdom.

TUESDAY, TWENTY-SEVENTH WEEK OF THE YEAR
Gal 1:13-24 and Lk 10:38-42

This story makes you wonder what acts of hospitality Martha was so worried about doing for Jesus. It probably had to do with preparing something to eat. Some people almost have an obsession about wanting to feed others when they come to visit. Generally, though, the most important thing is to first just sit and talk. After sharing friendship and conversation for a time, then refreshments could be shared. Of course, if someone were starving, that would be a different story. But we're usually not that hungry and, most likely, Jesus wasn't either. On this visit to Mary and Martha, Jesus seems to have been hungrier for conversation with his good friends than he was for food. Was it Martha's "Type A" personality that drove her to the kitchen, rather than to the feet of Jesus alongside Mary? When we say, "Let's have lunch together," the real message behind the invitation is, "Let's find a quiet place where we can sit down and talk for awhile." A major advantage of going to a restaurant instead of eating at home is that we don't need to be concerned about preparing and serving the food or cleaning up afterwards. It makes conversation so much easier. If Jesus were more interested in conversation than food, then Mary responded better to his needs. We frequently think only in material terms. This incident reminds us that spiritual needs are often much more important.

WEDNESDAY, TWENTY-SEVENTH WEEK OF THE YEAR
Gal 2:1-2, 7-14 and Lk 11:1-4

Today, we read that section of Paul's letter to the Galatians which contains his famous dispute with St. Peter. Since Paul is telling the story, we get the message from his point of view. We never do hear Peter's position. In essence, Paul publicly confronted Peter for discriminating against the Gentiles in favor of the Jews. It happened in Antioch, Syria, where Peter and Paul had met for only the third time. There was bitter tension between the Jews and Gentiles, especially over the question of circumcision. Peter was being very friendly with the Gentiles until some Jewish people arrived. He then ignored the Gentiles and associated only with the Jews. This angered Paul, but he remained silent. What caused him to publicly censure the first pope was that the other Jewish converts abandoned the Gentiles and even Paul's friend, Barnabas, followed their rude example. When we are sure of our facts, and know basic principles are being violated and innocent people are being hurt, then we, like Paul, have an obligation to voice opposition. This Christian duty of justice is to be followed even though we might be confronting some very important people.

THURSDAY, TWENTY-SEVENTH WEEK OF THE YEAR
Gal 3:1-5 and Lk 11:5-13

This is the story of The Midnight Visitor. It's meant to teach us how we should think about God. The image of God current at that time was harsh and cruel. We are to think of God, Jesus says, as a good and loving Father. The Lord presents these three analogies. (1) If your friend called you in the middle of the night and asked for something to eat, you couldn't just say, no, hang up and go back to sleep. Your night's sleep would be ruined by worrying about that hungry person. You would give what was needed. God does the same. (2) If a little boy asked his dad for a piece of fish, his father wouldn't give him a snake. (3) If a child wanted a hard boiled egg, a mother wouldn't give a scorpion or poisonous lizard instead. The very thought that a parent would act in such a manner is absolutely ludicrous. Jesus says don't think God would do that either. When we ask often and don't receive, we might be tempted to think that God doesn't hear or care about us. That's not true. God is not like that. Children, often, don't receive what they request, but it doesn't mean they're not loved.

FRIDAY, TWENTY-SEVENTH WEEK OF THE YEAR
Gal 3:7-14 and Lk 11:15-26

A person reading this Scripture passage from Galatians will notice five different sets of quotation marks. Paul has quotes in this passage from Genesis, Leviticus, two from Deuteronomy and one from the prophet Habakkuk. His purpose is to prove a point to the reader by listing a series of quotes from the Bible. The technique is known as "stringing pearls." Paul's point is that Abraham was a man justified in God's sight because of his faith and not his observance of the Jewish law. A person wishing to be justified by the law must keep the entire law. If any small portion of the law is broken, the entire law is broken. It was nearly impossible to live for a day without breaking at least a tiny part of the law, for the law had numerous prescriptions. Paul, a knowledgeable rabbi, found faith-justification much simpler and more honest. That was what Jesus taught and that's what drew Paul to abandon Judaism and accept Christianity. One doesn't have to be Jewish to be a child of Abraham, i.e., a child of faith. His first "pearl" explains how God intended Abraham's faith to be shared not only with the Jewish nation, but with all nations and all people for all times.

SATURDAY, TWENTY-SEVENTH WEEK OF THE YEAR
Gal 3:22-29 and Lk 11:27-28

Perhaps some of the pastoral procedures in the Church today as well as our own attitude toward the law might be reviewed against the background of Paul's letter to the Galatians.

Paul is hitting hard in chapters three and four to emphasize that faith in God is much more important than observance of the Hebrew religious laws. How do we juggle that delicate balance between the spirit and letter of the law? Galatians suggests that we may be too strict in these sensitive areas? The primary factor which is necessary for salvation is, as Paul says in this passage, faith in Christ. That, of course, implies obedience to his commands. "Not everyone who says to me, 'Lord, Lord,' will enter the kingdom of heaven." But it also implies that most other regulations are secondary in effecting justification. Faith in Jesus as Savior is to be our monitor, whether we are black or white, American or Asiatic, Protestant or Catholic, single or married. "Each of you," Paul says, "is a child of God because of your faith in Christ Jesus" (Gal 3:29). This trusting faith in Jesus is basic to our salvation.

MONDAY, TWENTY-EIGHTH WEEK OF THE YEAR
Gal 4:22-24, 26-27, 31 - 5:1 and Lk 11:29-32

Normally, the Pharisees were the ones confronting Jesus and finding fault with his teaching and ministry. However, here, Luke says the crowd was trying to challenge him. Shortly before this Jesus had cast out a devil and some of the people said he cast out devils by Beelzebul — the prince of devils. Others requested a sign from heaven to verify his authenticity. Again, the crowd confronts him by demanding a sign of his authority from God. We would suspect that the Pharisees were encouraging the people to challenge him. Jesus is caustic in his reply — calling this "an evil age" and saying that the people of this age would be condemned by the queen of the south and the citizens of Nineveh. They wanted to see something powerful and spectacular. His only sign for them would be neither. It would be a sign of defeat. He would be killed and buried in the earth for three days. He would show no sign to them except the sign of Jonah. His three days in the tomb, like Jonah's legendary three days in the belly of the whale, has become a symbol for all times. The real sign, of course, was not his being in the tomb for three days but his emerging from it on that first Easter morning. Today, whenever we hear or speak of the resurrection, we are reminded of the sign of Jonah, which Jesus promised to give.

TUESDAY, TWENTY-EIGHTH WEEK OF THE YEAR
Gal 5:1-6 and Lk 11:37-41

It seems we are born with a natural inclination towards the external. We tend to be superficial rather than profound. We, naturally, want to make a good appearance, dress well, talk and walk the right way, etc. Most people know us only externally. Only a few, relatively speaking, share the many thoughts which are swirling through our minds. Here, we witness Jesus telling the Pharisees they should pay more attention to their internal appearances. Religion is internal even though it may boast many external practices and ceremonies. In the liturgy we try to express internal thoughts and feelings through words and signs. Could we find the occasion today to ask someone about what's happening in their lives? We probably would surprise them, but they might appreciate the question and the opportunity to express themselves. Maybe, we could encourage them to speak of their fears, if they wanted to. Maybe we could discuss some recent book they read, what they think about the coming election, changes in the Church, or national affairs. Religion is within. Small talk is one thing and deep talk another. The Pharisaical person is an external person; Jesus is internal.

WEDNESDAY, TWENTY-EIGHTH WEEK OF THE YEAR
Gal 5:18-25 and Lk 11:42-46

Are you guided by the Spirit? You hope so, but how do you really know? Paul says there is a way to determine who and what actually directs our lives. If guided by the Spirit, there are certain qualities which openly manifest themselves in our everyday actions. We can think back over our recent days and see if these expected qualities were present. The list begins with love. It means that we care deeply for other people and want only the very best for them. Following that we should find in ourselves faith, joy, peace and patient endurance. These are personal qualities which give strength and tone to the very center of our lives. In spite of adverse circumstances, these virtues hold us together. If we show kindness, generosity, mildness and chastity, then we are living under the direction of the Spirit. These are positive qualities and the person who lives them possesses a tremendous inner strength. Thinking and acting in the opposite way is easy and very natural. There is nothing of the supernatural about it. The excellent endowments we possess show we have been advancing, developing and living Spirit-centered lives.

THURSDAY, TWENTY-EIGHTH WEEK OF THE YEAR
Ep 1:3-10 and Lk 11:47-54

The people of Ephesus must have felt elated when they received their letter from Paul. The thoughts expressed, however, are for a much wider audience than Ephesus. What is written is also for us. Today, in the first chapter we read a wonderful litany of blessings which God has bestowed on us through Jesus. Let us pray this litany with the response: Thank you Jesus. We are chosen — Thank you Jesus. We are predestined — Thank you Jesus. We are adopted — Thank you Jesus. We are redeemed — Thank you Jesus. We are forgiven — Thank you Jesus. Notice it says we were chosen before the world began. Paul implies here that the world was made for us. Since we were chosen, we had to have a place to live. Imagine, we were thought of and planned for before the world itself. After being chosen to exist, we were predestined to be God's children, adopted into the divine family, redeemed by the blood of Jesus. And we sinned. God's love didn't stop — we were forgiven. Don't we agree with Paul? " . . . so immeasurably generous is God's favor to us."

FRIDAY, TWENTY-EIGHTH WEEK OF THE YEAR
Ep 1:11-14 and Lk 12:1-7R

Whoever originated the statement about "killing two birds with one stone" was not very sensitive to birds. Why would we want to kill a bird at all? They are part of creation and a joyful part. Today's Gospel says not one bird is neglected by God. They provide the natural background music for the world. Although Jesus says each bird is beautiful and valuable, we as human beings are even much more precious. Our worth exceeds a whole flock of sparrows. We are so precious that the Lord was willing to give his blood and life that we would not be lost. Because God so loves us we should fear nothing. We shouldn't fear any person, for even if someone would kill us, that person could do no more. No killer can do anything to jeopardize our soul. So, ultimately, we don't need to fear the killer. We don't need to fear God, for we have been told how precious we are in God's view. As Franklin D. Roosevelt said, "There is nothing to fear but fear itself." "Fear nothing, then. You are worth more than a flock of sparrows." These words were spoken to the friends of Jesus. As long as we are listed among his friends, the above guarantees stand.

SATURDAY, TWENTY-EIGHTH WEEK OF THE YEAR
Ep 1:15-23 and Lk 12:8-12

In the Old Testament, Yahweh alone wanted to reign, but the people clamored for a human king. They finally obtained one, in the person of King Saul. He was found to be far from ideal. In fact, none of Israel's kings were totally satisfying to the demands of the office. The king had the dual responsibility to make the laws and to lead his troops into battle. He was given extensive power, for it was thought the more his power, the more ordered society would be. Paul sees Jesus as the King of the Universe. He is seated at God's right hand and is high above all the angels. God has placed all things under his feet and made him the head of the Church. We, the people of the New Testament, are fortunate to have such an ideal king. Jesus, alone, measures up to the ideal. He preaches peace instead of war and leads the people to achieve it. Paul, here, reminds the Ephesians of the glorious leadership of the Church in the person of Jesus. "God," Paul says, "has put all things under Christ's feet and made him head of the Church. . ."

MONDAY, TWENTY-NINTH WEEK OF THE YEAR
Ep 2:12-22 and Lk 12:13-21

"Avoid greed in all its forms." That statement of Jesus sets the tone of this Gospel. Greed is an excessive desire to possess more than one needs or deserves. The man in the parable was very rich and now another abundant harvest was placed in his lap. What would he do with it? We would have been very edified and God would have been very pleased if the rich man would have said, "I have enough for myself, I'll give this harvest to help the poor." Sadly, it seems, he never even considered it as one of his alternatives. His attitude resembles that of Ebenezer Scrooge, the greedy and avaricious character created by Charles Dickens. Visited by the spirits, Scrooge, finally, was convinced that there was more joy in sharing with others than hoarding everything for one's self. The rich man of the Gospel died clinging to his material possessions. God calls him a fool. May the spirit of Jesus live within us that we will find fulfillment in giving to others, instead of wasting our lives trying to grow rich for ourselves.

TUESDAY, TWENTY-NINTH WEEK OF THE YEAR
Ep 2:12-22 and Lk 12:35-38

Europe is not as "far away" from the United States as it used to be. Formerly, it was days or weeks away; now it's only hours. The miles separating the two continents are the same but the means to travel there have improved. Also, the degree of difficulty has been tremendously reduced. In that same sense, Paul tells the Ephesians that God is not as far away as he used to be. In former times we were hopelessly separated. Between us there were barriers of hostility, fear and superstition. The ways in which we tried to relate to God were confusing and cumbersome. All that has changed with the coming of Jesus. The old demanding laws, which were nearly impossible to observe in their entirety, have now been revised. The new way of relating to God is simpler and more direct. We now need only to have faith in Jesus, the great mediator. In the person of Jesus, the divine and the human have become one. This one person — Jesus — is the new link between heaven and earth. Our Lord Jesus is both the corner-stone and the capstone of the new temple, where divinity and humanity mingle.

WEDNESDAY, TWENTY-NINTH WEEK OF THE YEAR
Ep 3:2-12 and Lk 12:39-48

The last two sentences of this Gospel are worth a few minutes of our thought. The message is: the more that is given to us, the more will be required. There is a natural tendency within people to brag. Some control this urge and others give it free rein. We know who they are and we, also, know if we are part of the bragging group. It can be done very verbosely or subtly. As we tell the world of our good qualities and fine talents and blessings, we are, thereby, acknowledging we have a more demanding account to give to God. At judgment time the braggart may complain about God's decision, thinking it unjust. "Why should those people fare better than I?" he may ask. "I did just as much as they." But the Lord will answer, "You should have done five times as much. I often heard you say," Jesus will add, "how much better you were than they." Even if one does not brag, the saying still holds true. "When much has been given to a person, much will be required of that person. More will be asked of one to whom more has been entrusted."

THURSDAY, TWENTY-NINTH WEEK OF THE YEAR
Ep 3:14-21 and Lk 12:49-53

Paul is totally humbled in the Lord's presence when he thinks of the absolute magnitude of God. He kneels before the Father and prays as a sign of intense reverential worship. The usual position of prayer for the Jewish people was standing. We can imagine Paul on his knees, writing these words for us. Here is expressed a beautiful concept of the love of God, with four well chosen words — breadth, length, height, and depth. The author, Joseph Grassi, says these words were used in the Stoic philosophy, which was current and popular at the time, to express the totality of the universe. Paul is saying God's love is boundless; it supercedes the world and is a more valuable possession than human knowledge or any kind of material gift. The apostle is on his knees, with hands extended. He's trying to reach out to grasp the magnitude of divine love. He wants it all. Some churches have

included in their names the words, "Full Gospel." I never understood the necessity for adding that; it should be presumed.
However, this passage leads us into the full Gospel and the
fullness of God's love.

FRIDAY, TWENTY-NINTH WEEK OF THE YEAR
Ep 4:1-6 and Lk 12:54-59

This Gospel account expresses a bit of ancient wisdom
concerning the weather. When you see dark clouds arise in the
west, you can predict rain is on its way. If the wind is blowing from
the south, it will bring to us hot weather. We can analyze these
maxims today and understand their meanings. They are the
first-alert, visible signs of other factors which are yet hidden, but
will later be manifested. The weather, today, continues to be the
second most discussed topic. The first is our physical health (and
how the weather affects it). The point Jesus makes is, if we can
read the signs of the weather so well and accurately, we should
also be able to read spiritual signs. What, for example, is pre-
sently occurring within me which might produce favorable or
harmful repercussions in the future? There must be some clear
signs I can see right now that indicate the direction my life is
going. I can not see over the horizon but my signs function as a
heavenly mirror. They give me a high vantage point to look
beyond the scope of what can be seen by the natural eye. Our
future depends on both internal and external happenings. There
are signs for each. If the signs within us say tomorrow appears
dismal, maybe we can change our course.

SATURDAY, TWENTY-NINTH WEEK OF THE YEAR
Ep 4:7-16 and Lk 13:1-9

In 1943 Pope Pius XII issued the encyclical, "Mystici
Corporis," designating the Church on earth as the Body of Christ.

The term "mystical body" had been used with various interpretations since the 12th century. St. Paul speaking of this concept, calls the Church the Body of Christ. There is no place in Scripture where the Church is called a "mystical body," although the idea is present. In this passage Paul says the Church, with its many parts and functions, is similar to a physical body. All the parts of a healthy body function in unison with each other. The many parts are built around the various bones. We can't speak of bodily unity without mentioning the ligaments, which hold the bones of the body together. The real basic "bones" of the Church are the apostles who extend the original thrust from Jesus; the prophets who lead, working on the cutting edge of tomorrow, and the evangelists who bring in the new members. The pastors are the "bones" of the Church for they minister at the altar and keep alive the divine truths. Also the teachers, who help the young and old to understand and continue to learn. When all function in love and unity, we see the mystical body of Christ in our midst.

MONDAY, THIRTIETH WEEK OF THE YEAR
Ep 4:32 - 5:8 and Lk 13:10-17

When a person has a problem which weighs heavily on the mind, the body can also be adversely affected, especially if the problem remains for a long time. Mental worries, we know, will often publicly announce their presence in the form of bleeding ulcers. Prolonged sadness can cause acute depression and be clearly visible in downcast eyes and the diminution of strength and ambition. On the positive side, it's good to know that a person who has suffered mentally and physically for many years can have hope for a cure. In this Gospel, Jesus meets a woman who is heavily burdened with a problem. Luke, the physician, notes that it first had bent her mind and then her body. This had gone on for eighteen years, but now came the cure because she had faith to be healed. Jesus freed her mind and straightened her spine. Luke the doctor, was impressed nearly as much as the lady herself. Soon, at this Mass, Jesus will sacramentally touch us. By that touch, what do we need the Lord to heal or correct in our lives?

TUESDAY, THIRTIETH WEEK OF THE YEAR
Ep 5:21-33 and Lk 13:18-21

We have observed, experimented and noted how various things in the world act and react in given situations. We can predict the results of numerous types of reactions because of a quality known as consistency. We can predict that a pan of bread dough will quickly double its size because of the presence of yeast. When planted and nurtured, a mustard seed will multiply its size hundreds of times. Jesus says this same type of consistency exists in the spiritual realm. Like the yeast and the mustard seed, we can expand to become bigger and better today than we were yesterday. We do this by the presence of God's grace within us. It's in the nature of things to grow, whether it be yeast, mustard seeds or God's grace. We can observe what happens, but we are totally incapable of making it happen or giving it the power to happen. Our faith and trust in God is expected to be so strong and consistent that we, too, can be spiritually predictable. When a lie is convenient, we will be truthful. When a person's rights are violated, we will be vocal. When someone falls, we will help the person to rise. Christians are expected to be predictable.

WEDNESDAY, THIRTIETH WEEK OF THE YEAR
Ep 6:1-9 and Lk 13:22-30

There are thousands of books and articles about the relationships between parents and children. One fine book is *You're a*

Better Parent than You Think, by Raymond N. Guarendi, Ph.D. In the preface he tells parents, "This book is dedicated to your mental health." Guarendi's approach to parenting is simple and centered in common sense. In todays Scripture reading, the Apostle Paul preaches a brief and common sense-centered wisdom. He says, "Children obey your parents." We can almost hear the kids asking, "Why?" Paul says, "Because it is expected of you." That's a rather simple answer. Obeying parents is minimal. The children are expected to do more. "Honor your father and mother," he adds. Children won't always be bound to obey their parents, but they will always be expected to honor them. The apostle is not one-sided, though, for he adds that parents are not to anger their children, but to bring them up in the Lord. He doesn't rule out discipline, but does say that it should be administered with patience and love. Maybe we're all better people than we think, if we act out of love and common sense.

THURSDAY, THIRTIETH WEEK OF THE YEAR
Ep 6:10-20 and Lk 13:31-35

When he was told that Herod was trying to kill him and he should leave the territory, Jesus replied, "Go tell that fox . . . I will proceed on course." The anger of Jesus was evident but restrained. The fox has an ancient reputation for being wily and sly. Sometimes he's almost too clever and shrewd for his own good. When I was a child we had a pet fox named Oscar, which we raised from a baby. He was a manipulator, especially adept at finding his way into the chicken house and making a meal out of a little chick. It led to his eventual downfall. Occasionally he would be attacked viciously by a mother hen as she fought to protect her young. Here, Jesus compares himself to a mother hen protecting the baby chickens. The Lord wants to gather them under his wing, but they refuse. Notice how Jesus is comfortable comparing himself not only to a chicken but to a mother hen. Jesus, like a mother hen, is no "chicken" when fighting to protect the lives of his own. The Lord here is pointing out the tremendous strength of those living creatures which we normally think of as weak. We may be small and frail, but with God's strength we are a match for any foe.

FRIDAY, THIRTIETH WEEK OF THE YEAR
Ph 1:1-11 and Lk 14:1-6

Paul begins this letter to his very dear and personal friends, the Philippians. Their friendship was not love at first sight. Originally, the Philippians had persecuted Paul and tried to kill him. He forgave their hatred and lovingly continued to minister to them. This unusual conduct so favorably impressed the Philippians that eventually they wholeheartedly accepted Paul and he, them. His deeply personal and emotional love for them developed beyond that which he had for most other people. In the opening part of this letter, he says, "I think of you constantly . . . and hold all of you dear." Paul's experiences in Philippi can be a real source of inspiration and counsel for us. If we abandon a person or group because of an initial disagreement, even a serious one, we may be depriving ourselves of a most wonderful future friendship. Patience, tolerance and forgiveness are much more than spiritual words in a religious vocabulary. They signify a way of thinking and acting. Eventually, these qualities are to lead us into a total way of life full of blessings and joy.

SATURDAY, THIRTIETH WEEK OF THE YEAR
Ph 1:18-26 and Lk 14:1, 7-11

The Scriptures are filled with teachings about the earthly life and the eternal one. It's a basis for most theological teachings.

The first we accept because we observe it and know it is real. The second we take on faith because Jesus promised it. Some Eastern religions even teach that we have a third life — a pre-existing one. The very same circumstances which bring an end to one type of existence are the beginnings of a new one. Life is everywhere, in many different forms. Dying, therefore, is not a ceasing to exist but a change to a new kind of existence. Paul, in this passage, is discussing the merits of living and dying. It's his conviction Christ will be with him, whether he is living or dead. He can say, therefore, that dying is desirable for thereby he gains union with Christ. Living here is also appealing for then he can continue his productive work for Christ. It must give one a tremendous sense of security to be that confident about dying. What a blessing it would be if we could all have our spiritual values and temporal matters in such good order. Death then would have lost its sting for us, too.

MONDAY, THIRTY-FIRST WEEK OF THE YEAR
Ph 2:1-4 and Lk 14:12-14

In this Gospel, Jesus mentions some people who should be invited to dinner. The poor should be invited, rather than the wealthy. Included in the poor are the beggars, the crippled and the blind. We consider ourselves, no doubt, to be in the inviting category rather than those who are invited. It may be very sobering for us to realize that just the opposite is true. We are attending this eucharistic meal today. We are the invited ones — the poor. The host, Jesus, is following his own advice. We are the beggars for we come with our requests and prayers of petitions. Constantly, we ask, plead and beg with the Lord to satisfy all our needs and desires. We are the crippled. Perhaps not physically but certainly we are spiritually crippled. Wounded by original sin, we have frequently fallen and continue to stumble in an ongoing effort to keep our spiritual balance. We come also as the blind. Greed, avarice, passion and selfishness obscure the light and blind our judgments. We have all been invited to the king's table. Although we are unable to return the favor, the king understands and says that it's OK.

TUESDAY, THIRTY-FIRST WEEK OF THE YEAR
Ph 2:5-11 and Lk 14:15-24

This passage is, in reality, an ancient profession of faith. It tells the story of Jesus. He is God and came from God. Through the Incarnation, Jesus emptied himself of heavenly glory. More impressively, the Lord reduced himself to the level of a slave. He lived with the intention of dying in our behalf. When he took the final step, it was an extreme one. Jesus allowed himself to be treated as the most wretched of criminals and chose to die on a cross in the most painful manner imaginable. Then came the major turnabout. Jesus was exalted and all people of every tongue are to offer the Savior glory and praise. The conclusion is that Jesus Christ is Lord! This passage is too filled with faith and beauty simply to be read. It must be pondered for many long hours to derive its powerful message. That's the only way our attitude can become that of Christ. Most likely, this section of Scripture was an early Creed in the Church which the people may have known by heart. If we would like to memorize a few verses of precious Scripture, this would be a good choice.

WEDNESDAY, THIRTY-FIRST WEEK OF THE YEAR
Ph 2:12-18 and Lk 14:25-33

St. Paul, as a clergyman, voices thoughts which must surface in the minds of most clergy and those who minister to others in the faith dimension. In so many ways, the clergy try to inform people about the truths of Christianity. This is done in the schools and other classes, at the RCIA, in sessions before baptism, matrimony, and on numerous other occasions. People usually attend these but often do not follow with participation in worship or the fulfillment of other promises which were discussed and agreed upon. On the more favorable side, however, there are those who express thanks for the efforts of the clergy and continue to be faithful to their religious commitments. These are the "Philippians" in our lives. If it were not for them, many clergy might feel that they had "run the race in vain and worked to no purpose." Paul tells the Philippians he loves them dearly, wishes them many blessings and thanks them for their cooperative kindness. He was so impressed and grateful, for they were living the faith he had preached. Everyone needs to feel appreciated, clergy included and, in fact, even saints. Thank God for the Philippians.

THURSDAY, THIRTY-FIRST WEEK OF THE YEAR
Ph 3:3-8 and Lk 15:1-10

Imagine all the ways we can sin — in thoughts, words and in our actions. Some sins are very embarrassing and we don't want them to be known. Others may appear to be even humorous and we readily share them. Most sins are simply boring — yet all sins are wrong. Our transgressions of the divine law give us a title we don't like, but it designates what we are — sinners — all of us. In this Gospel Jesus is accused of welcoming and eating with sinners. The Lord doesn't deny the charge but openly states he truly does love sinners. He compares them to lost sheep, which a shepherd places on his shoulders and carries home. I imagine on his painful way to Calvary, Jesus blotted from his mind the label of being a criminal as he bore his rough and heavy cross. Perhaps he thought of himself as a shepherd carrying a wounded sheep on his shoulder. If we see our work not as drudgery, but as serving others, we will not think of people as sinners but as brothers and sisters. In that way we will be like Jesus.

FRIDAY, THIRTY-FIRST WEEK OF THE YEAR
Ph 3:17 - 4:1 and Lk 16:1-8

Paul sounds rather conceited in this passage, telling people to imitate him if they want to live in the proper way. We may ask, "Just who do you think you are to lift yourself up as a model of how Christians are supposed to live?" We know it's difficult to be a standard for others but when we consider the depth of dedication in Paul's life, we can appreciate the humility and truthfulness behind that statement. Paul sincerely attempted to live the complete Christian life and tried to do so every minute of the day and night. Who of us could feel comfortable in saying we imitate Christ twenty-four hours everyday? So, instead of judging Paul as conceited, we should view him as extremely dedicated to the true and full living of the Christian message. We would not dare to make such a claim, but wouldn't it be exciting if we lived such a dedicated life that we could give others that same advice? It is stated we are living in Christ if we don't set our hearts on things of this world, but recognize that we are citizens of heaven. There we are to find true fulfillment.

SATURDAY, THIRTY-FIRST WEEK OF THE YEAR
Ph 4:10-19 and Lk 16:9-15

Here, we have the conclusion of Paul's affectionate letter to his unwavering Philippian friends. He can't seem to thank them enough for their prayers and material support of him. He appreciates their gifts, not so much that he has received them but that they have offered them. The apostle says he has learned something which is very valuable — perhaps we could learn it also. He says, "I have learned how to cope with every circumstance." I heard an elderly preacher give a talk years ago, where he explained how his approaches had changed over the years of his ministry. As a young man, he tried to solve every problem he encountered. Now, in his later years, he said he was not trying to solve all problems but simply attempting to cope with them. Paul says it's fine if he eats well and is provided for, but he can also cope with hunger and material poverty. His coping is not with principles, but with possessions or the lack of them. This day many things will be not the way I want them. Paul will give me direction. I, too, can say, since God is my source of strength, I have strength for everything.

MONDAY, THIRTY-SECOND WEEK OF THE YEAR
Tt 1:1-9 and Lk 17:1-6

The tone in this letter to Titus is in sharp contrast to Paul's gentle words to the Philippians which we were reading last week. Here, he is speaking to his appointed bishop, rather than to the congregation directly. Paul is giving Titus some strict guidelines to be followed for establishing the Church on the island of Crete. The virtuous qualities of both priests and bishops are mentioned. These, Paul says, are the expected requirements of anyone in a leadership position. This same list of qualifications had already been given to another bishop, found in chapter 3:1-7 of the First Epistle to Timothy. You'll notice that the requirement of celibacy for priests did not exist in the early Church. Here, marriage and children are not considered a disadvantage to the priestly ministry, though St. Paul does state that "a presbyter must be married only once," meaning that if his wife died, he should not feel free to remarry. In verse ten, immediately following where today's lesson stops, the vices of irresponsible teachers are listed. Paul says they are empty talkers, they deceive and upset families. "They must be silenced." Chapter one of Titus gives the image of what a good Church leader should be. It tells one how to live and what to say.

TUESDAY, THIRTY-SECOND WEEK OF THE YEAR
Tt 2:1-8, 11-14 and Lk 17:7-10

One who is a servant is called to live in a certain way. Jesus explains what that way must be. Servants have designated duties, which are assigned to them and these must be accomplished. Servants do not decide if they will work or not, nor do they say they will do only a little bit because others aren't working. The family for whom they work, may be very busy or simply sit idle under the shade tree all day. Some of their fellow workers may be lazy and under-performing, but the good servant will continue to do his or her assigned tasks, regardless of what the others do. If we would substitute the word worker, in place of servant, we would get a clear biblical picture of what is required of us in our modern day society. There are many types of workers, but the guidelines apply to all. We should not look about to see what others are doing, in order to determine what we should do. When you do your job well, you should feel a satisfying sense of accomplishment but you should not expect a gold medal or a written note of congratulations for doing only what you were expected to do. Remember the Lord is our Divine Master and we are servants. Our duties to Church and religion are not based on how much others do, but on what the Lord tells us we should do.

WEDNESDAY, THIRTY-SECOND WEEK OF THE YEAR
Tt 3:1-7 and Lk 17:11-19

One day in religion class, a teacher was trying very hard to convince her first graders to act as Christians. Christians, she explained, obey the laws, work hard, and are kind to others. The children listened very attentively and she felt her talk had made a deep impression on their little minds. "Any questions now on the matter we just discussed?" she asked. One six-year-old girl raised her hand and asked in the fullness of childhood simplicity: "Teacher, do we have any of these Christians who attend our church?" Paul is telling Titus to preach to his congregation this same message about being obedient to the laws, working hard, and displaying courtesy to all. Paul is clearly reflecting on his own former life when he hated and persecuted others in the name of religion. He says we've all done our share of foolish and sinful things, but we have been forgiven through Jesus our Savior. We, like Paul, should be very impressed that God's mercy has been given to us — free of charge. If the little girl could see us, would she recognize a Christian according to the description given by her teacher? Hopefully, there are many Christians in our churches.

THURSDAY, THIRTY-SECOND WEEK OF THE YEAR
Phm 7-20 and Lk 17:20-25

Philemon was a prosperous young man who probably lived in Colossae and was converted to Christianity by St. Paul. He had a wife named Apphia and a son called Archippus. He also owned a slave named Onesimus. Onesimus ran away and came to Rome — a city which attracted many fugitives. There, he found Paul, whom he had met in Colossae. Paul gave him refuge and converted him to Christianity. Eventually, Paul encouraged him to return to Colossae and serve his master, Philemon. Onesimus was frightened to do so, for he had been guilty not only of flight, but also of theft. He envisioned a severe punishment from his master, if he would ever return. Paul insisted he should return, but to protect him from punishment the Apostle wrote a brief letter to Philemon. Onesimus was to carry it with him and to present it to his master on his return. This is the letter we read today. Tradition tells us that Onesimus was received by Philemon without being punished; in fact, he was eventually given his freedom. Later, this one time slave is said to have become the bishop of Ephesus. Can we tell the story of our journey from slavery to freedom?

FRIDAY, THIRTY-SECOND WEEK OF THE YEAR
2 Jn 4-9 and Lk 17:26-37

Our reading today is from the shortest book in the Bible. The reading contains only six verses, but that's nearly half the entire book. Although small in size, this Second Letter of John preaches a message which could not be greater or more important. It reminds us of the new commandment we have from Jesus, and the essence of that commandment is found in verse 5: "Let us love one another." There is an ancient tradition that when John, the last surviving apostle, was a very old man, people would continually ask him questions about Jesus and what he taught. John, it is said, would summarize the entire teaching of Jesus with the words, "Little children love one another." The word, love, is spoken millions of times each day and has taken on a million different meanings. In the basic biblical sense (especially the Old Testament), it means a voluntary attachment. This attachment, when applied to God, gives the concept of love its highest expression. Jesus said that this same voluntary attachment which we have to God is to be applied to other people. Love, then, would become the hallmark of a true Christian.

SATURDAY, THIRTY-SECOND WEEK OF THE YEAR
3 Jn 5-8 and Lk 18:1-8

Sometime ago *The Atlanta Journal* published the results of a research conducted by Professor Benjamin Bloom of the University of Chicago. He and his associates had studied top performers in different fields to determine what contributed most to their outstanding success. They studied individuals in science, medicine, literature, the performing arts, music, sports, business, etc. We might assume that these people had extraordinary talents in these areas and they simply developed them. The research showed differently. As children many of these individuals had done poorly in the areas in which they were now so very proficient. The common thread in each success story was determination and persistence. They had developed a drive to succeed and that enabled them to accomplish their purposes. The key element which made them successful can be summarized in one word — perseverance. The widow in this Gospel story would never have gotten a just settlement from the wicked judge, had she not possessed that precious quality of perseverance. She, too, is a real success story.

MONDAY, THIRTY-THIRD WEEK OF THE YEAR
Rv 1:1-4; 2:1-5 and Lk 18:35-43

Today, we begin reading the Book of Revelation. The title gives only a slight clue of the contents. It's former name, Apocalypse, was more descriptive of the nature of this last book of the Bible. All Scripture is revelation since it reveals and communicates divine truth. There are many types of revelations, such as, messianic, historical, moral, dogmatic, etc. This book contains apocalyptic revelation, which is characterized by symbolic imagery, imminent cosmic happenings and unrestrained grandiose predictions. This type of literature was very popular in Jewish and Christian circles especially from 200 B.C. to 200 A.D. In the book of Revelation, we are to expect the unexpected, to look for the symbolic rather than the literal interpretation of the text and realize that the complete message may elude us or be grasped only in a vague manner. The inspired thrust of the Book of Revelation was to remind the original audience that, even though they are suffering at the present, help is on the way. This assistance will come from God, so hold on patiently. For us, too, in our troubled times, this book can bring a reminder of the blessed message that hope springs eternal in the human breast of the one who believes in God and tries to keep his word.

TUESDAY, THIRTY-THIRD WEEK OF THE YEAR
Rv 3:1-6, 14-22 and Lk 19:1-10

Countless people are accused of all kinds of violations and are often sued in court. We know how much preparation must go into a court trial, and every precaution is taken lest an innocent person is condemned as guilty. Contrast that procedure with the many rash judgments we make about people. So often, with no real knowledge of their innocence or guilt and with absolutely no hard evidence, we accuse, judge and convict them and publicly broadcast our decision. Zacchaeus was a man unjustly accused of being dishonest. It was "evident" he was crooked because he was a tax collector and was rich. How do tax collectors get rich? The people said they steal the tax money. Some tax collectors did, it is true, but Zacchaeus did not. Another grossly unjust judgment concerned his small stature. Because he was short, they determined, he must be a very small man in every other way. Jesus, in this passage, is also judged to be a sinner because he associates with Zacchaeus. "He has gone to a sinner's house as a guest." While we ought to refrain from judging others, we can judge ourselves and should. It's very fortunate for us that Jesus is willing to go to the house of yet another sinner — and that house is ours.

The author of the Book of Revelation is eminently knowledgeable of the Hebrew Scriptures and the ancient formats of literary expressions. The Old Testament contains several visions of prophets before the heavenly throne. It was a common way for a prophet to introduce himself to the world and present his credentials. Since the prophet has experienced God's presence in heaven, he is not only well-qualified but also authorized to speak God's word to the people. Who would dare object to a truth which the prophet had actually experienced at the heavenly throne? This picture of the power and glory emanating from the heavenly epicenter also convinces the readers of this book that the Roman Emperor does not rule the world. The real source of power is localized in God — ruler of the Cosmos. The importance of Caesar and his military might is now miniaturized and the fears of the persecuted vanish amidst the cherubim, incense, hymns and the glittering imagery of heaven. The upbeat message of this passage gleams and sparkles with hope as brightly as the crystal clear floor surrounding the throne.

Jesus wept over the people in the city of Jerusalem because they did not know "the path to peace." It was not as though they were intently seeking peace and couldn't find it. At one time they understood, but now had "completely lost it from view." Destruction, pain and death will come upon them. God will not bring about their punishment, however. Rather it will come as a consequence of their own unfaithfulness. It's all the result of their refusal to walk "the path to peace." On what path are we walking today? Perhaps, Jesus is weeping for us too because of our deliberate choices to walk a different path. If we're not on the path to peace, we've lost our way and are not approaching the fulfillment of our lives. True peace flows out of our communion with God and with each other. It signifies a state of interior calmness, regardless of the pleasant or painful circumstances which may surround us. The more we bring love and joy into the lives of others, the more peaceful the path becomes for ourselves.

FRIDAY, THIRTY-THIRD WEEK OF THE YEAR
Rv 10:8-11 and Lk 19:45-58

The famous 17th century author, Francis Bacon, once wrote: "Some books are to be tasted, others to be swallowed, and some few to be chewed and digested." No doubt, Bacon would have recommended the Bible to be chewed, swallowed and digested but not literally. It is the mind and spirit which should gain strength from the biblical ideas. In this passage of Revelation, the angel hands the scroll to John with the instructions: "Here, take it and eat it!" John, literally, ate the message and then filled with the sacred words, began to prophesy. John is eating the scroll in circumstances similar to Ezekiel (Ezk 2:8-3:3). In both cases, dramatic statements are being made about God's word becoming a part of one's very being. Once the divine message is totally digested and absorbed, as it were, into the system, then the person is qualified to speak to others about the mind of the Lord. We are not to literally eat the pages of our Bibles but we are expected to assimilate their teachings. Those lessons will sometimes be sweet and sometimes bitter. Both are genuine and both expected; for it's all part of the total menu.

SATURDAY, THIRTY-THIRD WEEK OF THE YEAR
Rv 11:4-12 and Lk 20:27-40

Here is the famous passage of the very durable lady who wedded seven times and never had to change her married name. For her seven husbands, one might wonder if she were the kiss of love, or the kiss of death. All seven, who were brothers, married her hoping for children, which never arrived. But no one can accuse that family of not putting forth a united effort. What a brotherhood! The Sadducees told this story to Jesus trying to confuse him and discredit his teachings on the resurrection. "Whose wife will she be," they asked, "at the resurrection?" They then added, "Remember, seven married her." I wonder why they felt compelled to add the reminder that all seven had married her. I'm sure Jesus remembered it very well. The whole content of the story and its tone is an attempted put-down. Jesus calmly diffused their imagined cleverness with the statement that there are no marriages made in heaven. They originate and end on earth. The Sadducees, already depressed by their failure to believe in the resurrection, are now defeated again. Since they opposed Jesus, they couldn't win. That's why they were "sad," you see.

MONDAY, THIRTY-FOURTH WEEK OF THE YEAR
Rv 14:1-3, 4-5 and Lk 21:1-4

The Book of Revelation is literally filled with numbers which have many symbolic meanings. In this passage, again, we meet the 144,000 who are saved. These numbers are not meant to be taken literally. Numbers, as used in this book and in Hebrew thought in general, are more adjectives than quantitative numerical values. An often used number is 3, but it's meaning is vague in the Old Testament. The Holy Trinity has baptized 3 in the New Testament. In our modern usage, it expresses completeness when used in examples, stories, jokes, etc. The number 4 is a favorite of Scripture also. It's original importance probably came from the 4 points on the compass. It's number 7, though, which gets the most attention. That number is literally everywhere in the Bible and means fullness. Number 10 is also popular, the root of the decimal system. The often used 12 survives in the dozen. Number 40 is another prolific, quantitative adjective. It signifies a generation. Likewise, 12 x 12 equals 144, which was the number of military units in the ancient Israelite army. Therefore, 144,000 saved is not a limiting number but it means a tremendous multitude. It's good news about salvation.

TUESDAY, THIRTY-FOURTH WEEK OF THE YEAR
Rv 4:1-3, 4-5 and Lk 21:5-11

The story of Revelation continues to unfold as seen from a heavenly viewpoint. A white cloud appears out of the blue. Seated on the cloud is a person wearing a golden crown and carrying a sharp sickle, who resembles the Savior. Whenever clouds appear in the Hebrew Scriptures it is a sign of God's presence. In the book of Genesis, the rainbow appeared in the clouds as a sign that the human race would not be destroyed. It symbolized a new beginning under divine protection. In this cloud is the sign of the sickle. It symbolizes the end has come and now is harvest time. Both symbols are crescent-shaped and complement each other as two bookends, with earthly life held between. Here the word goes forth to harvest the wheat and the grapes for the final time. The good earth has produced the wheat and grapes a million times for human food and drink and for divine sacrifice. This, now, will be the last banquet and the final offering of bread and wine. Soon we can expect the voice from the cloud, and then there will be the fulfillment of all human life in the final transfiguration.

WEDNESDAY, THIRTY-FOURTH WEEK OF THE YEAR
Rv 15:1-4 and Lk 21:12-19

Here, Luke is predicting certain events which are associated with the end of the world. It is commonly known as his eschatological discourse. The exact time of the world's demise remains uncertain but more immediately is the coming fall of Jerusalem. The once proud Temple will crumble, people will suffer and die and Judaism will be changed forever. Both themes are interwoven. In sequence, Luke places this passage before the Last Supper, which for the followers of Jesus marked their last Passover Meal and the beginning of the new Eucharistic Liturgy. Invaluable divine protection is promised to those who remain faithful to Jesus. Outwardly, they will appear to be in dire jeopardy, but within they will be very strong and totally at peace. When faced with physical pain and mental suffering, they will be afforded the privilege of tapping directly into the divine wisdom. The passage concludes with the secret on saving our lives — patient endurance. It can be applied and lived immediately. If trust in God and patient endurance can enable us to survive the worst of times, they can certainly lead us through today.

THURSDAY, THIRTY-FOURTH WEEK OF THE YEAR
Rv 18:1-2, 21-23; 19:1-3, 9 and Lk 21:20-28

As the liturgical year is fast drawing to a close, the daily readings continue to emphasize the theme of completion and fulfillment. Here, the finale is viewed from an earthly point of view. In contrast to Tuesday's lesson from Revelation, seen from the heavenly perspective, Luke now focuses a close-up on the city of Jerusalem. He notes especially that pregnant women and those nursing babies will face severe hardships at this time. They will be bringing new life into the midst of a death scene. The imagery is sharp and descriptive. Frightened people will "fall before the sword." The citizens will "be led captive." The once proud Jewish sanctuary of Jerusalem will be "trampled by the Gentiles." Historically, all these happenings did indeed occur, and most likely many of the details were added to the biblical account after the fact. The second half of this passage returns to the theme of cosmic destruction as the end of the city and world are described in unison. These passages also apply to the personal deaths of each of us. It is faith in God's loving power and saving grace that will save us in the end.

FRIDAY, THIRTY-FOURTH WEEK OF THE YEAR
Rv 20:1-4, 11, 21:2 and Lk 21:29-33

When we read this section of Revelation, it is necessary to continually remind ourselves that this is apocalyptic literature. Recall again that the purpose of apocalyptic literature is to give hope to struggling people by convincing them that God is in charge. It employs symbolism, giving numbers adjectival qualities and speaking often in dramatic cosmic terminology. Therefore, we have to make it clear that though the text says the devil will be chained for "a thousand years," and then released for a short time, we must not take that literally. A "thousand years" means a very long time, and obviously it is. It is used as an adjective not a number. People will want to panic with the ending of the second millennium in 2000 A.D. as they did in 1000 A.D. Rest assured, we, ourselves, will bring more "hell" into the world than the devil ever could. The dragons we fight are continually present and we know what they are. In the end, true virtue will triumph over evil. The white, sun-rimmed cloud is still hovering against the blue sky, the symbol of God's abiding presence. It is a harbinger of blossoming hope for a new heaven and a new earth.

SATURDAY, THIRTY-FOURTH WEEK OF THE YEAR
Rv 22:1-7 and Lk 21:34-36

The renowned poet, T.S. Eliot, once wrote these incisive words: "In the end is my beginning." Today is the end of the liturgical year, which is concluded by reading the last chapter of the last book of the Bible. The thoughts of the heavenly paradise expressed are reminiscent of those ideas spoken in the first book of the Bible. It was in the Genesis account of the original earthly paradise that we were first introduced to the rivers, trees and fruit. It was there, too, we heard the unfortunate curse upon all humankind. But that was long ago and far away. In the meantime, the trees have grown and produced their fruit. The rivers have reached their oceans. The last long distance runner has crossed the finish line in the human race. Salvation history has been unfolded and humankind is restored to that pristine purity it once knew in paradise. Now in the end, there is a new beginning. The rivers are again crystal clear and the delightful fruit from the trees can be eaten without fear of any curse. Our original desire to "reign" is now fulfilled. The days are pleasantly warm and there is no night. What was lost in the beginning has been found in the end.